THE MEANING OF S

'An uproarious dictionary of style. . . . on each topic with entertaining vexation and gives refreshing proof that "fashion sense" does not have to be an oxymoron' *The New York Times*

'Deliciously off-message about the fashion world' *londonpaper*

'A punchy style bible packed with fashion advice about everything from lingerie to layering, models to make-up' *Tatler*

'A witty, humane and substantial survey' *Daily Telegraph*

'Proof, at last, that fashion can be smart and funny' *Harper's Bazaar*

'A witty, tongue-in-cheek demystification of the vernacular of fashion . . . Delivered with a perpetually raised eyebrow, this is a wry, philosophical A–Z that conveys fashion's delirium and delights' *Easy Living*

'An entertaining guide for the discerning fashionista' *Closer*

Hadley Freeman was born in New York. Despite not being wholly clear on why blue and green should never be seen, she is fashion and features writer for the *Guardian*, writes a weekly column for *www.style.com* and is a contributing editor to *Vogue*. She lives in London.

The Meaning of Sunglasses

A Guide to (Almost) All Things Fashionable

HADLEY FREEMAN

PENGUIN BOOKS

*For my parents, by whose sterling and collective example I
learned how to wear shorts and when 'i' goes before 'e'.
And for Kate Jones, who we all miss dearly.*

PENGUIN BOOKS

Published by the Penguin Group
Penguin Books Ltd, 80 Strand, London WC2R 0RL, England
Penguin Group (USA), Inc., 375 Hudson Street, New York, New York 10014, USA
Penguin Group (Canada), 90 Eglinton Avenue East, Suite 700, Toronto, Ontario, Canada M4P 2Y3
(a division of Pearson Penguin Canada Inc.)
Penguin Ireland, 25 St Stephen's Green, Dublin 2, Ireland
(a division of Penguin Books Ltd)
Penguin Group (Australia), 250 Camberwell Road, Camberwell, Victoria 3124, Australia
(a division of Pearson Australia Group Pty Ltd)
Penguin Books India Pvt Ltd, 11 Community Centre, Panchsheel Park,
New Delhi – 110 017, India
Penguin Group (NZ), 67 Apollo Drive, Rosedale, North Shore 0632, New Zealand
(a division of Pearson New Zealand Ltd)
Penguin Books (South Africa) (Pty) Ltd, 24 Sturdee Avenue, Rosebank, Johannesburg 2196,
South Africa

Penguin Books Ltd, Registered Offices: 80 Strand, London WC2R 0RL, England

www.penguin.com

First published by Viking 2008
Published with revisions in Penguin Books 2009

1

Copyright © Hadley Freeman, 2008

The moral right of the author has been asserted

Book design by Janette Revill
Set in ITC Berkeley OS Book
Printed in Great Britain by Clays Ltd, St Ives plc

A CIP catalogue record for this book is available from the British Library

ISBN: 978-0-141-03199-6

Everyone who is smart says they hate fashion, that it's such a waste of time. I have asked many super-serious people, 'Then why is fashion so popular?' Nobody can answer that question. Miuccia Prada

I probably own thirty pairs of white jeans. I'm just obsessed with them. Elizabeth Hurley

Preface

*A*h, the handy historical quote: friend to all expounders on subjects based more on personal opinion than on scientific, objective fact. And so, let us commence this new edition of *The Meaning of Sunglasses* in that fine tradition with just such a handy peg. As Coco Chanel (yeah, I know – you saw that one coming) once said, 'Fashion is made to become unfashionable.' This is not just a convenient truth for designers who need to convince people that what they promised to be life-changingly fabulous six months ago is now irretrievably horrendous and must be replaced with their latest even *more* fabulous wares el pronto. It is also an ominous warning for anyone who dares to write a book about fashion. Take heed, oh plucky style writer: you may feel ever so canny, tip-tip-tapping on your super-skinny Apple Mac, rolling out pronouncements about which nail-polish brand is de rigueur and why aviator shades are always a reliable classic, but such words will bite you in your Power-Plate-toned backside in six months' time, you mark my words.

Unlike the cleverly temporal fashion magazines, which can make their didactic statements about what is 'good' and what is 'bad' safe in the happy knowledge that they'll all be recyclable pulp in 30 days' time before any of them can be held accountable, fashion books have a peskily tenacious way of hanging around for at least a couple of years. Thus, that tone of inviolable rectitude that the writer adopted when blithely explaining why green is good and yellow is bad sounds a little less impressively imperious when – quelle horreur! – yellow has since become the colour of the new season, according to Balenciaga and Prada.

Since this book first came out last winter there have, of course, been some changes on the sun-dappled fashion landscape. The biggest has probably been the freefalling world economic situation, which has certainly affected people's shopping habits, although no one seems sure yet whether this means people are buying more super-cheap clothes, or buying more expensive clothes as – to use the favoured term – 'investments'. Some of us might suggest that perhaps the surest sign of economic worry would be people not buying anything at all, although, as anyone who has had the misfortune of finding themselves on the high street on a Saturday afternoon can testify, this does not seem to be happening quite yet.

Speaking of super-cheap high street clothes, the other big development over the past year is the seemingly weekly revelations about which Western high street retailers depend on the sweat and blood of Indian and Chinese children to make their goods. All these exposures are accompanied by the requisite horrified gasps of customers. Now, people – come on. To continue to buy clothes that cost about the same as a pack of gum, and then to express shock that they were not woven by contented couturiers, hand-sewing the goods while reclining on satin quilts in a Paris atelier, seems more than a touch naive. Someone is paying the price for these clothes. And seeing as it's not the customer and it's unlikely to be the store (most stores tend to be a bit reluctant to sell clothes for less than they paid for them

– they're funny like that), then perhaps it's someone else. Someone around the age of ten, maybe. It's like those diets that promise you can eat stuffed-crust pizza and double-chocolate fondue and still lose weight. Life just doesn't work that way.

This is not to argue that the only kind of clothes you should buy is couture, which really is made by quilt-reclining couturiers. But just as the best way to eat is to have a normal-sized amount of half-decent food – not Michelin-starred, and not greasy, battery-farmed off-cuts – at reasonably spaced intervals, so the best way to shop is to buy the occasional piece of well-made clothing. Not Versace, perhaps, but something that costs more than a pack of Maltesers.

But what about the trends, you cry? Well, yes, there have been some changes there, too. Ballet pumps have now been superseded by loafers because, well, apparently some blonde model wears them and, um, so does some TV presenter. So there. Skinny heels are making an inevitable comeback and, oh yeah, red is very, very 'in' at the moment (perhaps reflecting the world economic situation. Or perhaps not.) As for what's coming up in 2009, gird yourselves for exaggerated shoulders, harem trousers and eight-inch-high heels. But, really, this book was always built on personal opinions as opposed to insights into upcoming trends, and no matter how many times some of us see photos of Agyness Deyn wearing her loafers, we have yet to be persuaded that they are anything other than the footwear of Sloanes and middle-aged geography teachers. Although fashion is routinely criticized for being an industry that stuffs pointless opinions into certain people's otherwise empty skulls, personally I always found that it only made me more sure of the opinions I already had. There ain't nothing like seeing endless photos of some pop singer's girlfriend wearing clunky flat shoes, and being told ad nauseum by gossip and fashion magazines across the land that they represent the pinnacle of 'edgy style', to make one slip that little more smugly into one's delicate ballet pumps.

There are now so many voices out there screaming about 'what's viii The Meaning of Sunglasses

hot' and 'what's not'; rare is the celebrity, music or film magazine, or TV show that doesn't feel the need to add its two bits to the fray, to say nothing of the continually growing fashion magazine market. Frankly, only a person who wore at least 973 garments at one time could incorporate everything that they were told was 'in' into their outfit, and then they might look more homeless than fashionable. There comes a point when the overload of opinions about what to wear tips you into realizing that the only ones you can really rely on are your own.

This book never meant to offer advice on anything so personal. Instead, it's a guide to what it means when someone wears a polka-dot coat, why mittens are offensive when worn by anyone born before 1999 and why the hell people who buy 'vintage' are so damn smug. These basic, unarguable, stand-alone truths of course remain as true today as ever, thus making this book as impervious to the whims of fashion as a Viking warship standing tall and uncowed by the rolling seas around it. Though it goes without saying that loafers are always, always wrong. Obviously.

Introduction

*I*n one characteristically if particularly prescient episode of the TV show *South Park*, originally aired back in 2004, Paris Hilton arrives at the animated eponymous town in Colorado to open a store, marketing her distinctive look to the mountain-bound eight-year-old girls. Now, leaving aside the aesthetic merits or otherwise of this concept, this raises some interesting questions: is it, as one character claimed, 'empowering' to encourage girls and women to dress in a particular style or does it, as another stoutly put it, turn you into a 'stupid, spoiled —'? And there, for decency's sake, we must abruptly stop quoting from *South Park*, but you probably get the idea.

Of course, this question is fairly easy to resolve about dressing specifically like Hilton, but in regards to fashion as a whole it is, judging by the arguments exercised by some with the kind of tirelessness that would impress a Russian Olympic athlete, more complicated. Is fashion one big nasty anachronistic and misogynistic conspiracy to make women feel inadequate, or is it a means of self-expression that brings a lot of pleasing gratification?

If one were to go by the way fashion tends to be covered in the media, well, it's not looking so good. One popular approach in upmarket publications is to make commendably po-faced announcements that a certain £1,300 handbag is a 'must have' and that the only permissible style of trousers this season is drop-crotch jodhpurs. At the other end of the fashion magazine scale, one finds fashion commentators who make getting dressed into a kind of logic puzzle: one long torso plus two short arms equals a V-neck top with a bias-cut skirt, and if you fail to know these rules you will live your life in solitary frumpish purdah. For those of us who can barely remember how to use the coffee maker in the morning, the thought of having to master this kind of sartorial mathematical equation before work is enough to make us want to cash in the New Look gift vouchers we received for Christmas and curl up in a burlap sack.

But if you look at how women in this country relate to fashion, it's a very different story. Thanks largely to the rise of the high street, with a special bouquet going to Topshop, and also to the crop of young designers who have emerged over the past two decades, particularly Marc Jacobs, Miuccia Prada, Comme des Garçons' Rei Kawakubo, Stella McCartney, the former designer for Chloé, Phoebe Philo, Nicolas Ghesquière and Luella Bartley, fashion is more than ever for the women themselves, not the men who look at them. It is surely no coincidence that the majority of the designers listed above are women, as was the person behind Topshop's rejuvenation, Jane Shepherdson.

With regards to the impact of the high street on fashion, never before have so many good clothes been so readily available, so cheaply, and never before have so many women been in the position to buy them with their own money. The clothes on the high street are a far cry from the itchy boob tubes, bagging jeans and other pathetic excuses for clothes the stores shamelessly sold in the eighties. Instead, a woman can buy a fantastically smart work suit at Zara, and pick up a tunic dress that makes her feel fabulous at the same time. Go into Topshop on a Saturday (not something I would normally recommend – save your sanity and wait for Sunday) and you will see gaggles of giggling teenagers and pairs of grown women, silent with concentration, diligently flicking through beautiful blouses and more than decent dresses, admiring themselves in the mirror and paying their own money for things that make them happy. Some might see this as some kind of nightmarish vision of materialistic hell, but, unless I missed a crucial lesson in History GCSE, the Western world is not under communist rule and it is still permissible for a woman to buy something, just for her, that gives her a little smile of pleasure when she sees it in her wardrobe the next morning.

The response to this argument is that the only reason for the pleased smile is that the fashion press brainwashes women into believing they have to buy *that* dress and need *that* clutch bag for their personal happiness, and thus, any satisfaction is artificial, transient and conditioned. It's an interesting contention, and one that would

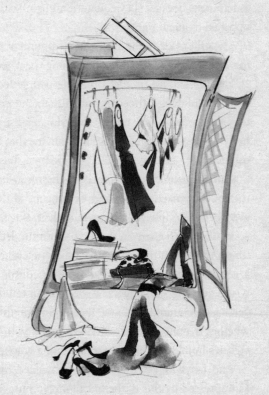

almost be worth responding to if this argument didn't also usually take the tack that women are childlike dullards who just don't
know their own minds, bless them, and need to be protected from
big scary *Vogue*, which, like a villainous bounder, is stealing the life
savings from doddering and gullible females across the land.

There is more to a woman than what she wears and how she
looks – of course there is. But I just do not see that having a sharp
brain and strong self-esteem is incompatible with caring about how
you look, and deriving pleasure from it. Surely the latter at least is
something to be encouraged. Aside from the fact that a little dash of
narcissism is human nature, to argue otherwise is what has led to a
whole generation of young women refusing to describe themselves
as feminists because they equate 'feminism' with excess body hair as
opposed to equal rights.

The other side to the anti-fashion argument is that if it's not making women too happy, then it's making them too miserable.

Fashion should be about making people feel good about themselves: confident, attractive, individual. But somewhere along the
way it accrued some rather annoying parasitic concerns, namely
body obsession. It is a real blinking shame that fashion, which exists
ostensibly to give women self-confidence, has become something
that many people see as precisely the opposite. Without question
the industry needs to expand its concept of the physical ideal, or,
even better, to lose its obsession with it. But seeing as that doesn't
seem likely to happen in the next – hmmm, let's see – decade or so,
it's up to women themselves to make the choice: either you can let
a few preening designers and fascistic editors ruin what is otherwise a very enjoyable pastime, or you can tell them to go jump and
get back to thinking about the important things in life, such as
whether a mini puffball skirt will make you look like a fabulous
eighties homage or like you're wearing a whoopee cushion.

And, anyway, I'm not entirely convinced that women feel quite
as oppressed by this as the fretful media purport. Think of some of

the most successful trends over the past few years: tunic dresses, ballet pumps, leggings, shorts, empire-line dresses and tops, clumpy wedge shoes, boots over jeans, handbags so large and ornate they could probably be used by NASA as base camp on Mars. These are clothes that are fun to wear, but are guaranteed to make no one look thinner or taller and, judging by the huge swathes of ladies who cheerfully vacuum-packed themselves into skinny jeans recently, women don't seem to mind. Whereas fashions of the past always seemed to have some kind of wearisome ulterior motive – shoulder pads in the eighties to make one look butcher in the workplace, wasp waists in the fifties to create a vision of the female form that pretty much rivals Barbie in its distance from reality – women today, with the occasional Hurley-esque exception, dress more than ever in a style that this book shall pithily describe as Clothes That Boys Don't Get But Girls Do. Sometimes this is to their aesthetic advantage (I refuse to believe that spinning gaily on the dance floor in a loose tunic is less attractive than a woman painfully winched into something that restricts any movement more extreme than squeaking out a plaintive bleat of pain), sometimes it's not (yes, shorts and tights do make a woman look like she is mid-performance of a transgendered *Hamlet* – I'll grant you that one). Either way, it is a marvellous retort to yet another patronizing argument that women are unable to separate the fantasy of fashion magazines from the reality of their own lives.

Finally, despite the often baffling imperative tone that dominates fashion – red? Good! Blue? Bad! – it is, of course, a wholly subjective pursuit. This kind of bossiness, I suspect, is part of the reason why some women still find fashion frighteningly offputting. Sweep past the naysayers and have faith in your own taste: all that matters is whether you like it or not. For anyone out there who might still feel qualms, this book will selflessly, fearlessly demonstrate the proof of this tenet. This is by no means an exhaustive guide to the fashion world. It is one built wholly on personal biases and bugbears, as opposed to detailed descriptions about how one should wear which accessory and to what occasion. Sometimes, yes, those kinds of tips can be helpful. But, after a while, I suspect, they simply suck away the little confidence some women already have in their own sense of style.

There are plenty of books out there that give the extensive biographical details of every single designer who ever sat behind a Singer sewing machine; instead, this guide restricts itself to talking about one designer or label for each of the fashion capitals who, for various reasons, best represents that city: Marc Jacobs for New York, Topshop for London, Prada for Milan and Karl Lagerfeld at Chanel for Paris. Some might disagree with those choices, some might even disagree with the choice of fashion cities, what with Bombay, Shanghai, Berlin and Madrid all eagerly stepping up to the plate. But then some might also disagree with this book's beliefs that fur is wrong, wedges are right and that anyone over the age of five who wears anything from Gap Kids is deeply, deeply suspect. How passé can you get?

Accessories, *going to hell in a handbag*

*O*nce upon a time, in a far away land, where fat trout lapped in babbling brooks and apple-cheeked maidens blushingly accepted bouquets from chivalrous squires, the fashion world was mainly about clothes. Now, as anyone who has given themselves a lifetime of orthopedic bills due to their Brobdingnagian large bag knows, it's almost entirely about the accessories.

The reasons why more women will spend £700 on a Chloé hand-bag than they will on a Chloé dress are well known (sing it as one, sisters: a-bag-never-makes-you-feel-fat), and their appeal to design-ers is equally simple (in three words, they sell faster).

And it's not just about bags. Every season there seem to be more little trinkets, ranging from Chanel camellia brooches to Miu Miu faux-school badges, and one can only applaud the designers' in-genuity.

Fashion has never been just about the clothes, as the long ven-eration of Chanel handbags proves. Never before, though, has it been quite so much about the hors d'oeuvre instead of the main meal. Once accessories operated, as perfume and make-up still do to an extent, as a compensating taster for those who wanted a bit of designer-label action, but couldn't afford to commit to a full-on relationship. But now accessories themselves have become just as expensive as the frocks because, as designers have learned, there really are some people out there who will pay £500 for a Marc Jacobs knitted hat.

Even at the less extreme end of the scale, the appeal of accessories leads one unavoidably to some rather ugly human truths. Namely, they flash the cash that little bit quicker. Swinging about a giant handbag decked with an undeniably pointless padlock will send a certain message – I Can Afford Chloé – a lot faster than if you just wore a pair of plain Chloé trousers. Logo names are far too obvious and therefore vulgar, whereas a whopping great lock and key which serves absolutely no purpose other than to shout the bag's origins is quite the height of good taste even if it does make the damn thing weigh about the same as a small car – and that's before you've put anything in it.

We can blame the high street for this to an extent, because now that it has become so good at knocking off designer clothes it is harder to justify buying that Marni smock when you know the high street will have a near-as-dammit one at literally one-twentieth of the price. Accessories – well, handbags and shoes, anyway – are harder to copy, particularly if, as designers have cleverly spotted, the It ones of the season are decked in chain, buckles and silken threads strung with priceless Japanese sea pearls (an exaggeration may lurk therein, but the essential truth is unchanged).

Those of a more philosophical bent have propounded some interesting theories on how the rise of accessory hardware reflects the growing international unrest in this century and, um, general sense of insecurity and, um, so it's like we're arming ourselves and, um, yeah. Personally, I love this idea. So all those Marc Jacobs chains, Mulberry buckles and Anya Hindmarch rivets aren't indicative of being a fashion victim

– no, we're doing our bit for our country, to free those hearts and minds! Yeah! Yet one cannot help but wonder whether this attempt to claim that our materialism is carried out in the name of international aid and Dubya's great cause might put women off the bags in a way that the price tags don't seem to do.

The simple fact is that a good-sized chunk of the general populace wants to flaunt their financial expenditure. Thus, we'll buy all the tunic dresses we like at Topshop et al, but, you know, a lady still wants the world to know that she can lay out the occasional £800, right? If anything, the contrast between the designer accessory and the high-street clothes ups your fash cred, because it shows that you may have money but you spend it judiciously.

None of this is in itself necessarily a bad thing: if having that handbag or those pair of shoes makes you happy, then why the hell not, it's your money and, as already said, if you're going to spend serious cash it really is better to do it on the accessories as the ones on the high street are much less cop (see *Money, and when to spend it*). And, heck, there are worse ways to show off one's wealth, such as having a customized car licence plate or making small children in Columbia harvest drugs for you.

Yet there is something a tad self-deluding about this buying of accessories, but shying away from the clothes. It's like believing that any food you eat while standing up and cooking doesn't count, so you shovel down the handfuls in the kitchen and then don't eat anything on your plate. Instead, you might as well just forgo all the little bits and save up enough for a Chanel jacket – or its calorific equivalent, the quattro formaggio – and have done with it and accept that you are as much of a fashion sucker as the next run-of-the-(tread)mill Wag. Yes, designer accessories may be better made than high-street ones, but let's not kid ourselves that all those extra chains and buckles and locks and contrasting threads are there for purposes even approaching practical.

One interesting point about accessories is just how clever designers have been at reinventing the wheel – or at least suddenly inventing some extra spokes heretofore unnecessary to your wheel's motion. Take the 'key fob', for example, which became very popular a few years ago thanks to younger labels such as Marc by Marc Jacobs and Luella. This, to the eyes of the ignorant, is merely a key chain by another name. But, ah, they are overlooking three crucial differences: 1. It's not for your keys, but rather to clip on to your oversized Mulberry bag, meaning that your £1,000 handbag now needs its own accessories. It does mean that the word 'key' in the name is a little misleading, but it is compensated for by the unexpected accuracy of 'fob' because they were, a cynic might argue, fobbed off on the public. 2. Key chains have tacky, airport-souvenir stand associations that are just unacceptable to a designer. More acceptable, though, is how lucrative these little kinds of knick-knacks can be. So with one single word alteration the once unbearable has been rendered crucial. 3. They're about ten times more expensive.

The rise of accessories has intriguingly coincided with the increase of designers and decent clothing shops in general, leading one to believe that maybe, after all, we have reached a point of having enough dresses, a surfeit of trousers, just that one too many tops that go-well-with-jeans. But a Louis Vuitton feathered beret? A Marni key fob? A Hermès muff? How have you never noticed that gaping hole in your wardrobe before? Charge it!

Advertising, *how it spins the fashion axis*

With perhaps the exception of the fashion assistant who knows how the invoicing system works and where the key to the fashion cupboard is, no one has greater power in the fashion world than – any guesses? No, not the designers, bless your idealistic soul. The editors? Stop it, you're bustin' my ribs. The models' nutritionists? Nice thinking out of the box there, but no. It's the boringly be-suited, sweaty, balding, utterly uninterested in anything to do with looking stylish, advertising execs.

This is not some rant against the stultifying capitalist world in which we live because, to be honest, it beggers the ability of any reasonable being to sustain this kind of idealistic, socialist-ish argument in regards to an industry predicated on flogging pretty bits and bobs. But being interested in the bits and the bobs does not mean that one must be so daft as to not know that the reason you bought them has more to do with the powers of Saatchi & Saatchi than Dolce & Gabbana.

If you have managed to retain a hold on some sweet innocence and happen to have a free hour or so, try this fun experiment: go through a magazine and count how many adverts for each brand appears and then count how many times those brand names are mentioned in the magazine, either in articles or fashion shoots, and then lean back and marvel at how they tally. In short, a magazine with an advertisement for, say, Prada on the back cover, is a magazine that's going to be featuring a lot of Prada in its shoots, maybe with an interview with Miuccia thrown in for good measure.

This is known, in the industry parlance, as 'showing support', as in, 'You didn't show us enough support last season, so we're taking our annual £2 million advertising account elsewhere. Have fun picking out what to wear in the dole queue, suckers.'

This is why you will never read anything negative in a fashion magazine, except, of course, if it's talking about something from last season and even under those extreme circumstances designers' names will not be mentioned, par example, 'Layers, out! Armani's frills, in!' And so, somewhat improbably, fashion magazines are actually the most cheerful publications on this planet and should probably be prescribed to depressives instead of Prozac for they are lessons in how to see only the good in something, even in the frilliest of situations.

It's not just the advertisers' money that keeps the mags in thrall: good advertising makes a magazine look better. A nice advert for Lancôme featuring Kate Winslet is going to make a magazine look a little more chic than one for Stanna Stairlifts or a mini porcelain re-creation of Stow-on-the-Wold. And seeing as a large part of a fashion magazine's articles and fashion shoots are, as everyone's mother has pointed out at some time, indistinguishable from advertising, it's a wonder that no one has put out a magazine of just adverts, reeled in the cash from not having to pay for any journalists, editors or photographers, and chortled all the way to their off-shore tax-break private island.

But the relationship is not wholly one-sided and here things get a mite complex. Advertisers are as dependent on the cachet of the magazine as the magazine is on the cash of the advert. To see an advert for Balenciaga in, say, French *Vogue* carries a slightly different intimation, or – to use the advertising lingo – level of credibility for the brand than if it was forced to plop itself in, say, *Take a Break*. So despite actually funding the publication, advertisers know how much they need the scabby editors and their poxy little magazines and God help us if they don't resent it. Aside from the gushing copy and presence in fashion shoots there are all sorts of other forms of signs of respect required from the magazine editors: lunches with PRs, general obsequiousness, enforced attendance at even the most dreary of fashion shows (see *Fashion shows, Darwin in motion*) and attending 'press days', at which you are presented with a rail of the very same clothes you just saw in the show and, bringing back memories of school presentations for which you did not prepare, are forced to comment on them. These, along with the general puffery that makes up so much of fashion writing, are the very things that give fashion journalism a bad name and all of which are because of, yes, advertising. So fine, this is a rant against advertising, albeit a suicidal one as it is conducted in the knowledge that without adver-tising much of the fashion world couldn't afford to exist. But, hey, even suicidal socialists are allowed to be well-dressed.

Animal print, *when women roar*

*C*ontrary to what your mother told you, an outfit's level of tackiness has nothing to do with hem heights, heel inches or skirt tightness: it has to do with the obviousness of the mes-sage. Granted, the aforementioned three factors can convey certain insinuations at loudspeaker level, but that is not the whole story. For example, a very tight but elongated (say, mid-calf level) pencil skirt mixes its messages and is therefore very classy in a, like, totally McQueen / Hitchcock heroine kinda way, whereas a super-tight, super-short miniskirt will have men asking if you charge by the hour.

The lesson here is that you should never underestimate your au-dience. Many women do this frequently when they get dressed in the morning. We have long gone past the point of just undoing that extra blouse button and entered into the generation of sloganned T-shirts. Girls, if your T-shirt has to say it, you ain't it, and if it has to say it twenty times, you never will be.

Animal-print clothing is even more grating because the message is simultaneously so embarrassingly obvious and so cringingly stu-pid. Yeah, we get it, babe – you're just wild, you are. In the sack, yes, yes. Like on the Discovery Channel – *we got it!*

If the print is on actual fur, well, that is, at first glance, just about forgivable because that is how fur looks so to complain seems churl-ish. But then this mood of tolerance is swiftly pushed aside upon the realization that the woman is wearing fur, and this takes the concept of unacceptable to a whole new level (see *Fur, bad, and definitely a little bit Nazi*).

But to see a lycra dress dutifully printed with all those black dots in desperate emulation of a leopard's skin, in a manner vaguely akin to a raddled lookalike insisting she is the spit of her chosen ethereal icon, is to see in action the definition of the phrase 'wasted effort'.

You can hold up as many photos of Kate Moss in her snow leopard jacket or leopard-print silk slip as you like, but you are doing nothing to argue your cause: Mossy looks good in anything, that's why she is a M-O-D-E-L (see *Models*), though, in fact, to some of us even she struggles to look like anything other than an undersized Godzilla in her beloved fur. The rest of us resemble craggy ol' gin soaks propping up the bar in the local Slug and Lettuce, occasionally goosing the local boys and telling the snickering youths how all the men in town were once after our virtue.

Anti-*ageing*

*I*n this super snazzy, techno happy, come-and-watch-a-brain-transplant-on-my-HD-TV-while-I-download-some-bootleg-Japanese-manga-films-on-my-iPhone age of ours, we like to think we've come a long way from the superstitious leech-happy middle ages. The fact that the skincare industry rakes in billions of pounds a year proves we have definitely not and frankly it's a miracle we no longer tie women over forty to a stake in the town square and burn them (we're much more sensible: we just ignore the old crones). In the seventeenth century doctors informed their trusting patients that draining the blood out of their wasted bodies would rid them of their bad humours; in the twenty-first century we believe a C-List celebrity when she tells us that a pot of white cream made partly from whale sperm but mainly from a load of chemicals will literally 'reverse time'. That's progress, baby!

Skincare suggests many perfectly commendable things: curing acne, resolving rosacea, simply giving your face a good scrub. But none of these seem quite exciting enough to explain the monolithic skincare industry. Skincare is so huge that it is often the supporting scaffolding of a fashion house, sopping up debts incurred by an unprofitable clothes division, it being much easier to convince the punters to shell out £30 for a pot of gunk than £1,800 for a tweed jacket. Yet the tweed jackets gives the brand name its vague fashion allure which in turn sells the gunk, even though you wouldn't really want that grannyish jacket if you could afford it in the first place. Don't think about this too long or the entire fashion skeleton will develop osteoporosis and crumble.

There are only four things in this world that make people spend collective billions: more money, power, sex and a promise that they will look better (i.e. thinner or younger). Obviously, you will only get the first three if you attain the fourth, so guess which people seem to care about most these days? Skincare is now a euphemism for making oneself look younger, just as detox is a fancy word for posh dieting with an extra £20 for a bunch of organic carrots instead of a 99p calorie counter (see *Yoga, detoxes and other euphemisms for exercise and diet*).

Why we all care so much about looking young is a bit of a puzzle. Going back to ye olden times comparison, this veneration of the young was understandable, mainly because if you reached thirty you were pretty much knocking on heaven's door so women had to get themselves knocked up asap to continue the human race. Now that a lady can have a child when she's fifty-eight if she so wishes and we're told there are too many of us around anyway, this not only persisting but increasing hysteria about the value of youth does seem a little odd. The press continues to make happy hay on a slow news day by printing a photo of someone in the public eye from twenty years ago next to one of them today showing that they – no, it cannot be! – look twenty years older. Time has passed! Hold the front page!

Maybe it has to do with that irksomely childish if endearingly reliable human trait of always wanting something that you cannot have. Or maybe we are all living in the movie *Logan's Run* and no one noticed because Michael York is, disappointingly, yet to be spotted running around town with an amulet. Or maybe it's because we're foolish enough to have been brainwashed by a money-grabbing beauty industry eagerly grasping after our gullible dollars. Who can say?

Happily, the skincare industry has stepped up to this much-needed plate, flogging pots of God knows what to the desperate public, like a medicine man proffering worm claw and cats' nipples out of the back of a covered wagon to a sad country town riddled with an uncurable plague. In 2005 America alone spent over $660 million on products that promised to hold the key to that holy grail: anti-ageing. Now ask yourself if Americans are looking any younger these days.

And speaking of seemingly youthful Americans, plastic surgery and Botox are a whole separate issue in that there is no faffing about with pretty euphemisms here, no pretending you're just 'looking after your skin': we're talking 'Get the scalpel out, doctor, and slice my cheek off' levels of bluntness here (see *Plastic surgery and how all those 1950s horror B-movies weren't so far off the mark*). Botox is rather like hard drugs in that it may have the immediate desired effect, but this is only short-lived and you'll find yourself on a treadmill of injections, having to top yourself up with annoying frequency. The fact that you can't make any facial expression is another deterrent, though not as much as that it is heavily advocated by Princess Michael.

The very phrase 'anti-ageing' gives the game away that this must be the most fruitless cause since Ukip. It brings to mind, funnily enough, the chosen slogan of the anti-abortion lobby, Pro Life; although as the genius that was Bill Hicks once said, if they were all so pro life, instead of picketing hospitals maybe they should protest against cemeteries. A similar point could be made about this anti-ageing malarkey as the only thing that will stop anyone looking a day older than they did yesterday is – insert drum roll – death. Yet cosmetics companies remain oddly averse to the idea of signing the Grim Reaper, preferring instead to choose currently resting representatives from the acting community. Although considering that moisturizers are made from a load of alphabet-heavy chemicals, most of which will probably turn out to be highly carcinogenic and ultimately fatal, maybe they are on to something here.

Bags, *a word or ten thereof*

*T*hat women love bags is a fact for which the fashion business gives a collective hallelujah to the God of capitalism on a daily basis (see *Accessories, going to hell in a handbag*). Why they love bags is for pretty much the same reasons they love shoes: they don't make you feel fat, you don't have to get undressed to try them on, size is either a non-issue or simply not related to your stomach and they don't necessarily suit Kate Moss any better than you, all of which is basically saying the same thing in four different ways. Women try to justify this love affair with high claims about 'being able to use a bag more than you would use one dress'. This claim loses its currency somewhat when you're buying your sixth handbag. Furthermore, surely this is more true about, say, a coat, but coats have yet to send women into apoplexies of pleasure in the way that bags do (see *Coats, stuck at the nexus point between dull and stressful*).

So if the bag has become a statement then one is duty bound to decode their individual meanings. After all, if a woman spends £1,200 on leather goods the least one can do is try to figure out what she is trying to say, other than, of course, 'I've spent over a grand on something in which to keep my dirty Kleenex and my Oyster Card.'

Because you have to hold a structured handbag in, as the name does suggest, your hand, this is an accessory that screams, 'I never have to carry my own shopping! Valet service all the way, baby-cakes!' Thus, to the majority of the human race, they are of no use whatsoever (see also *Clutch 'bag'*). You want to carry home more than one load of groceries? Outrageous! Not with the bag which will take 50 per cent of your available hands out of commission, you won't. You will spend your life trying to shove that mean little strap up your lower arm in an attempt to liberate your hand, but your victory cannot be but short-lived. Now you will have to walk with your arm all crooked and visual comparisons will come to mind of yourself with the Queen. Thus you are forced to surrender to the tyranny of the handbag.

Satchel bags are very useful for pretending that you are Ali McGraw circa 1976. But despite that indisputable advantage, there is a downside in that they are one of the many garments on this planet that are not for anyone who has had the temerity to have grown themselves a pair of breasts. (Hippy chicks didn't have breasts. They were too busy making daisy chains to grow them. This is why there is not a single item of clothing from the late sixties to early seventies that accommodates them. The good reader is referred to the contemporary works of Yves Saint Laurent and Ossie Clarke, not to mention the veneration of the young Mia Farrow, should they require further proof.) Thus, like the blouse (see *Blouses, not so librarian now, are they?*) they work best for those who use theirs to carry home their French pre-GCSE homework as opposed to BlackBerrys and office work. You can just let the satchel dangle down as opposed to crossing it over your chest, traffic warden-style, but it will bang against your thigh something chronic and you may as well just hand your wallet to a passing pickpocket and have done with it.

So make like Goldilocks and get one with a strap that is not too short, not too long, but just right, i.e. one that can be shoved up on to your shoulder or gripped in your hand as the day's whim takes you. Don't be an idiot and get one in suede or cotton or canvas or whatever kind of non-waterproof fabric. A bag you have to worry about getting dirty is as stupid as shoes you cannot walk in.

What designer you opt for says even more about you than the style, which is veritable proof that we have long since left the land of practicalities when it comes to bags and entered a world of statement making. Because designers can have more fun with bags than clothes, due to not having to worry about inconvenient things like women's bodies, the bag, more than any other piece of fashion, is used to solidify the brand's image. Bags communicate these kinds of signals to those who care about them faster than clothes because, simply, they are more extravagant, more ostentatious and often more expensive.

Chloé's Edith and Bay bags might look at first like the kind of thing Miss Gooch might have shoved in her bicycle basket in *The Wizard of Oz*, but their message is the same as that of the brand's younger-looking Paddington: namely, that the customer is (or fancies herself to be) a young and sassy lady who probably lives in some very cool loft with her very cool boyfriend in the city, but just loves to go riding at Mummy's on the weekends. Maybe she bought that battered bag on Portobello, maybe it's a legacy from her grandmother, the Countess of Snootyshire. More likely, she coughed up a grand and bought it on Bond Street.

Fendi, on the other hand, with its sharp and shiny logos, is about frighteningly well-groomed and even more frighteningly well-monied continental ladies who use words like 'chinchilla' and 'arctic fox' on a daily basis; Mulberry is for women young enough to believe that seventies Britain was one long Timotei advert in which they romped through the fields with Lady Debo née Mitford and this leather bag will let them relive it. Thanks to the genius of Karl Lagerfeld, Chanel bags now send multiple signals: either, I am a trashy starlet being ironic, or, I am a lady who lunches at Le Caprice and I still think it's 1986, or, I know my fashion history and I only accept the best (a.k.a. the most expensive). Contrary to industry belief that multiple signals dilute appeal, Lagerfeld actually just tripled his potential customers, and that's why he is the Kaiser (see *Lagerfeld, Karl, and why he's so brilliant*). These brand images are created in part by the look of the bags themselves, but also through a combination of advertising, magazine puffery and 'product placement', i.e. celebrities are given the bag for free.

You can find perfectly decent bags on the high street, but they tend to look like they're made either for thirteen year olds or her Maj herself and this is yet another reason why more and more women are forking out for designer handbags. Plus, you probably will give your bag more of a battering than you will, for example, a summer dress, so it is worth spending a little bit more on something that is well made and won't fall apart after three outings and one rainfall. So, yes, there is a smidgeon of a practical justification here. But only a smidgeon, mind.

As for men, despite designers and men's magazines' best attempts the man bag has never really caught on, not least because of the name's almost offensive stupidity, but also because the majority have to be carried (see, again, *Clutch 'bag'*). Rucksacks are only permissible if you are at a music festival, under twenty-five or Australian, ideally all three. Briefcases are fine, if not exactly the wildest option in town, and as for a computer bag, well, that is just sooooo late nineties. So embrace your lack of mammaries and get a handy little satchel bag which for some unfair reason won't bestow you with the hippy connotations. Not that there's anything wrong with hippies, of course, peace, love and all that. But we're talking about bags here, OK? And some things just obviously take precedence.

Ballet pumps, *twee versus comfort*

*T*he trajectory of a trend from Moss to mass to verboten is both swift and cruel. To recap, Kate Moss wears something, she gets photographed, the world trembles with excitement, the high street rolls up its plagiarizing sleeves and – bada bing bada boom – what was once so maverick now reeks of the stale stench of D-list celebrity photo ops and sullen teenagers on Oxford Street (see *Moss, Kate, and how she ruined your wardrobe*).

Ballet pumps were always going to be the archetypal victim of this sad descent due to the Gorgon-like curse of (a) looking very good on Kate Moss; (b) being extraordinarily easy for the high street to copy but (c) rather trickier than you'd think to do well.

When Moss was first photographed wearing them a few years ago, ah, how she brought back the memories, which we shall re-cap here in not particularly zeitgeisty Guy Ritchie fast-editing form: Hepburn! Bardot! Gamine! Skinny cropped trousers! Bang! Stone the crows! Cor!

Anyone who hasn't been blinded by the ingenuity of this astonishingly brilliant technique will have noticed that the common denominator to all of the above is a requisite for slimness and, as ballet pumps – a footwear invented for, lest we forget, the not-exactly-girthsome-demographic of ballet dancers – show, just because something emphasizes a skinny person's svelte-ness does not mean it will make everyone else look thin, a truth which the success of skinny jeans proves has yet to be understood.

This doesn't actually matter a pin: after all, if we all looked like Kate Moss then we wouldn't be quite so thrilled by photos of her looking a bit spotty with whatever boyfriend she's hanging with, and what a poorer world that would be. And to be honest, a curvy woman trotting about with a smile in a pair of simple flats is a far more attractive sight than a twiglet limping miserably in stilettos, but we'll get back to that in a bit.

Because it's not rounded calves that have proven ballet pumps' downfall, but their cheap imitators. Despite their apparent simplicity, ballet pumps are very easy to get very wrong. In fact, the simpler the concept, the easier it is to do badly, as pretty much every spin-off

TV show has proven, with the noble exception of *Frasier*.

The perfect ballet pumps have delicately rounded toes: not squat and wide ones like the cap of a mushroom, but ones with a gently rounded point. The soles should be thin and can be either soft or, for a more formal (and longer lasting) look, hard, which is a style that the company French Sole have made their own. They need to be narrow as otherwise you will look like a little duckling padding down towards the pond and they should cut away just under your toes. Always go for solid colours, though be wary of red as people will keep asking you if there's no place like home, and be careful about metallic because if you wear gold ballet pumps with black tights someone might mistake you for a grand piano, which is awkward for both parties.

In other words, the ballet pumps should look as much like – ooh, what a shocker – proper ballet pumps as possible. The originals really are the best, that's why we ripped them off in the first place (see *Classics with a twist*).

Squared toes, thick soles, rain-damaged tips, gratingly girly colours and patterns of the hot pink polka dots, little animals and shooting stars variety have decimated ballet pumps' once proud, understated Left Bank chic image. Truly, shoes with cartoon kittens on them have never crossed the threshold of Café de Flore. Instead, ballet pumps have become the simperingly twee, waterlogged alternative to trainers.

Having said all that, the ultimate reason the world took to ballet pumps is because they are really, really, really comfortable, a factor all too rarely found in the world of women's footwear. With the exception of trainers and the occasional flat boot they are the closest women have come to finding an acceptable shoe that gives them an insight into what it feels like to be a man and to be able to walk with nary a limp nor risk of blood-letting. Admittedly, they do suffer from weather-dependent issues but still, as (possible) ballet pump connoisseur Meat Loaf once so wisely said, two out of three ain't bad.

Bathing suits, *and how so little can reveal so much*

There is a general belief, propagated primarily by daytime TV shows and women's magazines, that the reason beach holidays are, to use their favoured term, so 'stressful', is because of the body exposure. Considering both of these forms of media are aimed primarily at women it's interesting how poorly they understand their audience. Certainly the first day on the beach can be a little 'stressful' if you have any neuroses about your body, pasty skin or surplus body hair. But pretty much by lunchtime you realize that, actually, the beach is a fantastic leveller. Forget about religious pilgrimages or dawn epiphanies: there ain't nothing like a day on the beach to restore your faith in an omniscient and wise Creator. Almost no one has a perfect body, and no one really cares. There they all sit in the beach café, tummies hanging over their waistbands, happily asking for extra ketchup with their fries. For heaven's sake, you spent all this money on a holiday, are you really going to waste it by angsting over something magazines insist on calling 'love handles', a.k.a. skin? Moreover, those who do have perfect bodies and have yet to experience the novel sensation of their bum rubbing against their mid thighs are almost invariably so unappealing in some way that one cannot help but pity them, not envy them. If they are male, they will almost always be utterly stupid, dull or vain, those being the necessary qualities for a man bothered to cultivate the body beautiful, who will spend the day obtrusively walking up and down the beach in the apparent belief that this is a very subtle way to garner admiration (this is one of the disadvantages of being stupid: you always underestimate your audience). If you are a woman, you will either be so heavily composed of plastic that you will have to hide indoors from the midday sun otherwise risk looking like the Wicked Witch of the West, post Watergate; or you will be on the arm of a cigar-chomping hairy beast who definitely does not have a perfect body and people will secretly refer to you as 'the geisha' behind your back; or you will be very stupid and will annoy everyone on the beach by talking loudly on your mobile about your latest colonic and going to the Sundance with Jude and Orlando. Or possibly all three. Yes, God is good.

The fact is, body issues on the beach aren't really that stressful because there's nothing you can do about them, and once you realize that you have no power over a situation things become a lot simpler. It's one thing when you have clothes on because then you can do some judicious covering, should you be so inclined. On the beach, you just gotta let it all hang out and be Zen about it. The fact that most women choose to wear a bikini instead of a one-piece pretty much suggests that, at least on the beach, maybe women aren't quite as neurotic about their bodies as is generally assumed. The fact that most women also look better in the former proves that they are absolutely correct not to be so, and perhaps all the fuss about having a flat stomach isn't quite as important as one has always been led to believe.

Choosing what to wear on the beach, however, is a trickier matter because here you do have control. Designer swimwear is obviously for people who have no intention of swimming (see *Exercise clothes, the new couture*) and that makes sense: there'd be little point in going Gucci if people can't see the 'G' logo because it is submerged under water, right? Bathing suits with comedy cutouts are just funny. Aside from the obvious tan line issues, it's one thing to have some cheeky cutouts on a long demure evening dress, but when a woman's in a bathing suit and the rest of her body is pretty much on display anyway, somehow getting a triangular-shaped view of her lower ribs, say, doesn't have quite the same impact.

A woman in a one-piece bathing suit is either a professional swimmer, someone with serious issues about the state of their belly or a lady who was traumatized by a missing bikini top incident in the past and has never been back since. If you reside in any of these categories, fine, just make sure you get a swimsuit with defined cups at the top as one-piece bathing suits flatten you down so effectively you could be in one of the many Shakespearean plays in which an actress, for plot reasons rarely explained to a satisfactory degree, has to pretend to be male. String bikinis are for the very confident and the very flat-chested (i.e. plastic trophy girlfriends and models on holiday); for everyone else, a bit of support is always welcome, as the Samaritans might very well say. Unusually, the fashion compromise for bathing suits actually works quite well: the tankini – basically, a waterproof vest top with matching bottoms – gets the best of both in that you get a bit of tummy coverage without the breast bind and is therefore a sign that the wearer might have a few body neuroses but she is not going to let them ruin her holiday.

Occasionally you'll get lobbed with the recommendation to wear a bikini with a slightly frilled skirt attached to the bottom because this will hide 'a multitude of sins', an occasional piece of cheese being obviously on a par with murder, adultery and coveting your neighbour's (non-dimpled, presumably) ass. However, the obviously infantilizing nature of this garment does, most sentient human beings might have thought, somewhat contradict pretty much any other potential benefits. 1950s-style bikinis, which are cut higher on the tummy and lower under the bum – are often recommended for similar reasons and, again, there is logic here. That you can also let your bikini line go for a little bit longer with these swimsuits is another benefit, albeit one rarely mentioned by *Vogue*. They do, however, make one resemble a wartime pin-up and you may feel like you should be pictured straddling a nuclear bomb and painted on the side of one of the Allies' planes.

Black is obviously the most flattering colour for swimwear. It is also, incidentally, the only colour bikini you almost ever see Kate Moss sporting, making one wonder for a few schaudenfraude-freighted happy moments if maybe she isn't that hot after all, considering she clings so neurotically to slimming back. However, while

Kate might not see a beach holiday as that big a deal, seeing as she seems to be on at least one every month, the rest of the human species probably wouldn't mind marking the occasion with a colour a little more celebratory than such a funereal shade. Solid colours are recommended simply because you won't tire of them as quickly during your bathing suit's lifetime (average lifespan: six summer holidays – nine if you can really stretch the elastic out).

Because the canvas is much smaller, so to speak, any messages thereon come across that much stronger and louder. Thus, a leopard print bikini is unacceptable unless you are starring in *The Return of the Sixty Foot Woman* (see *Animal print, when women roar*); one piece bathing suits with odd wavy lines around the waist area to give an illusion of slimness are about as subtle as Tom Cruise's gurning grin, and any superfluous details – dangling chains, tassels, belts – are the equivalent of check-in baggage for a weekend away: unnecessary extras that will weigh down what should be a simple, hands-free affair. Have fun on the beach, by all means, but maybe best to restrict that to the pina coladas and wave jumping instead of pink Pucci bikinis with full-length tassels.

Best-dressed lists, *the myths and the madness*

$\mathcal{F}$ ashion magazines are, it hardly needs stating, compiled according to the most rigorous scientific and mathematical formulae, with every theory and statement repeatedly tested by independent adjudicators to ensure that everything printed, from the new crucial trouser length that month to whether Sienna's latest haircut is any good or not, is God's only truth.

But the annual best-dressed lists, those cheap page fillers of which magazines are ever so fond, do perhaps have a touch of the subjective to them. At least countdowns in other fields – music, for example – tend to have some kind of backing figures behind them.

Even the magazine editors would agree: after all, they cry, they're only stating their opinion. But it's what this opinion is regarding that is the sticking point. As any reader knows who has ever been baffled by some of the old stuffy old Sloanes that get lauded in these lists, and why when one starlet wears a certain dress it's good but when another wears the same frock it's bad, this editorial opinion has much less to do with the clothes than it does with the people wearing them.

The main boon of the best-dressed list for a magazine is that it is a remarkably easy way to suck up to someone who the editor would like to interview one day (hence the enduring popularity of Jemima Khan and any young woman dating a member of the royal family), to justify to readers in advance next month's cover star (the reliable presence of the latest Bond girl, or yet another Rolling Stone offspring), or just feature people who make pretty pictures (any model). It is also a very good way to slag off anyone who has had the gumption to turn down an interview from the magazine or who shares an agent with someone else who has done just that. So far, not much to do with the clothes, then.

But then, being well dressed today doesn't have much to do with the clothes anyway. Most celebrities who get lauded with the title can't seem to get dressed full stop, let alone dressed well, seeing as they have a stylist on their daily payroll. Not so much best dressed, then, as best picker of a decent stylist, which, admittedly, doesn't make quite as snappy a coverline. The fact that Kate Moss does manage to figure out for herself which Bella Freud jumper should go with which Superfine jeans on a daily basis is often reported in tones of awe one might expect for news that the model were able to decode the Rosetta Stone.

But no matter because if magazines love these kinds of countdowns, the general public loves them even more.

Britain loves countdowns in general. This is, lest we forget, the country that is currently on number 115 (approx) in the Now That's

What I Call Music series. This is very much a greatest hits country:
forget the floating indie chaff, bring on Guilty Pleasures.

It's not that anyone really cares, or even remembers, who *Snobby
Snob* or *Wow!* magazines decree to be the best-dressed chicken in the
coop (respectively, the two Kate M's, Middleton and Moss) it's just
yet further proof that an increasingly large part of fashion's appeal to
the public is to see it worn by good-looking people with recogniz-
able faces. The use of the countdown gives this national obsession a
kind of competitive, even Roman justification, as though we are not
just looking at twelve pages of exciting people like Anna Friel and
Peaches Geldof walking various red carpets to parties celebrating the
launch of a new mobile phone, but rather the conclusive word on a
year-long debated point, even if that point is whose stylist wangled
the best clothes out of the most fashion press offices.

Black, *the new and the old*

*O*n one of the many instances in which the fashion world is
like the masons (the rituals, the odd personalities attracted
to it, the vague feelings of disdain towards the general public), the
members within have certain tests with which to ascertain who is In
and who is Out. Heel heights, trouser cuts and other telltale fashion
signs are, of course, all quickly perused upon the initial encounter,
but the surest way for someone to show that they are outside the
sacred circle is to abuse the industry's mother tongue (see *Fashion
speak*) and the biggest abuse of all is to talk about The New Black.

Non-fashion people love this phrase because it combines a useful hyperbole with a pleasing bit of nonsense while simultaneously
mocking the fashion world's reputation for factually impossible
non-sequiturs. Thus, it is most commonly used in news stories discussing the popularity of something unexpected, as in, 'Cycling: it's
the new black' and 'Are the Miliband brothers the new black?'

This cliché may have once been coined by someone in the fashion world, but it is now almost never used by anyone in it. Partly because they have been shamed out of doing so but largely because they know there will never be another black. Ah, blessed shade, that makes you slimmer, goes with everything and is also just a little bit scary – glory, glory be. Oh, fools who think any colour could ever stand in its stead!

Certainly the fashion industry is always looking for another way to get people to spend their money but even they know that claiming magenta is the new black will not convince anyone to dash off and buy four pairs of £150 magenta trousers from Joseph. Instead, they'll just tell you it's 'the colour of the season', thereby acknowledging that you will only be fooled into wearing them for six months at most before those catcalls of 'Oi, Bozo! The circus left town yesterday!' from the kids across the street begin to sink in.

And, anyway, does anyone want a new black? Some of us feel that there is too much black around as it is with far too many women dressing themselves in shadows for our post-feminist liking. As a wise sage once said, if everybody looked the same, we'd get tired of looking at each other, and some of us definitely do. So sod the black, and sod whatever the new one is and get out there and wear your magenta trousers with pride! Yeah!

Blahnik, *Manolo*

*L*ike 'Tampax', the word 'Manolo' has practically become a generic term in itself, although he perhaps would not be overly thrilled by the comparison. Venerated by the fashion cognoscenti, immortalized by *Sex and the City*, Manolo Blahnik's shoes are a rather strange proposition, being either innocuously plain (if you're looking for a pair of all but invisible strappy sandals, why then, my dear woman, look no further, and have your £450 at the ready) or

insanely over the top. This is because Blahnik has determinedly retained total independence, unlike many of his contemporaries who
have taken the conglomerate shekel and sold out to the big fashion
groups like LVMH and the Gucci Group, and therefore can do as he
darn well pleases.

The main reason Blahnik enjoys such fame and adoration is
because his shoes are so improbably, if admittedly only relatively,
comfortable. It's about the placement of the (generally very high)
heel and the angle of the instep, which should follow that of your
foot. This will hold your foot in place instead of letting it slip to
the bottom, jamming your toes at the tip and forcing all the weight
on to the ball of your foot. The heel, meanwhile, should be placed
at such an angle as to allow you to put some of your weight back
into it. Otherwise, one ends up with what is known in the business
as the stiletto strut, where the woman's hips are back in a different
postcode from her legs because all of her weight is forced forward
and she is trying in vain, vain being the operative word here, to find
her centre of balance.

Moreover, Manolos last for absolute ages which, yes, you would
hope for from a shoe with a £400 plus price tag, but is most certainly
not something you can take for granted from designer shoes. Thus,

the success of Manolo Blahnik provides us with a surprising insight into perhaps the truth of much of the fashion industry and the people who work in it: they may look all scary with their high and mighty pointy shoes but actually they are as prone to aching arches and heel breakages as, to use Elizabeth Hurley's endlessly fascinating term for people who aren't her, Elton or Hugh, 'civilians', and get just as narked off when the heel splits and they have to take it to Timpson's. And the fact that Mr Blahnik is single-handedly keeping alive the ducktail coiffure is yet another reason to stand and applaud.

Blouses, *not so librarian now, are they?*

*N*ot, of course, that there's anything wrong with librarians. But with the memorable exception of Marian the librarian in *The Music Man*, this is a profession that has not accrued particularly seductive associations and nor, until recently, has the blouse. This poor garment was a victim of, first, film stereotyping when it became wardrobe shorthand for mousey little repressed secretary ('buttoned up', you see – clever!), followed by trends prejudice: it was too old-fashioned for the youthful sixties, too starchy for the floppy seventies, too delicate for the shoulder-padded and sportswear eighties and too fussy for the grungy nineties. But the Naughtiest, as we are reluctantly forced to call this decade, has yet to decide on its adjectival epitaph, and so the blouse has managed to slip back on in there.

Chloé can take a lot of the credit for this because this brand showed that, actually, the blouse is as unexpectedly flirtatious as a fantasy convent girl. Unlike a boring old T-shirt, you can play with its near-but-still-modest transparency, either by wearing a vest beneath it or a respectable bra, ideally without deodorant stains; you can adjust the cleavage factor thanks to the buttons, meaning it is perhaps one of only four garments on this planet that really can be worn, to use that much trumpeted but rarely true phrase, day to night (the others being, as most women have figured out, a wrap dress, good jeans and decent boots); it looks a lot smarter than your average top, and it often looks better untucked, meaning you get tummy coverage without the slob factor.

Yes, well, hurrah hurrah, thank heavens for the resurrection of the blouse, lah di dah, what took us so long, et cetera and so on. Well, painful as it is to admit but our ancestors in the eighties and beyond weren't wholly unevolved in their thinking, despite living in the Mesozoic age. The blouse ain't brilliant.

Don't get one in a sepia hue or with some kind of old-fashioned haberdashery pattern on it – you think you're making an ironic fashion statement, in fact you just look like Miss Marple (and while we're here, a word about 'ironic' fashion statements: irony is a tone that is best delivered orally, not visually. Thus the majority of 'ironic' fashion statements tend to look pretty literal as opposed to cleverly sardonic. Unless, I guess, you spend the whole day walking around with your tongue lodged in your cheek but that might become a bit of a strain after an hour or so and eating would be nigh impossible).

Next, it has to be worn right, and this means, to continue the above point, not too literally. They look best with jeans as these keep a firm but friendly grip on the blouse to stop it from falling on to the stuffy side of the fence. You can just about get away with one with a pencil skirt, but for the love of heaven don't then get excited and slip on oversized fishnets and stilettos as you yourself have now fallen on the 'ironic' side of this apparently dichotomy-dividing fence. Short-sleeve blouses look nice with miniskirts or beneath short cotton dresses, but beware of tweeness, and a simple way to avoid this is to not get blouses with Peter Pan collars, which are slightly smaller than normal ones. A grown woman has no business wearing something with such a childish name (refer to kitten heel section in *Heels, the highs, the lows and when fat is better than thin*).

But the biggest problem with the blouse is you. Well, your bust anyway. This is not a garment made for breasts, which is why for the past forty years the blouse's demographic tended to be the under twelves – even librarians only wear them in films. It also explains why so many designers have become so fond of them as many of them do seem to find things like hips and breasts intolerably intrusive on their Art. Few things make a woman's breasts look more like a threatening cliff-like single mass than a thin blouse stretched out over them with an almost visible grimace, buttons pulling apart in palpable pain. So in this case the A-cups win and don't begrudge them too much because they deserve to get their kicks where they can. I mean, would you rather a blouse or a bust? Two words: consolation prize.

Boots, *the normal kind with a couple of variations*

*R*emember when boots were just there to keep your legs warm? I know! Hilarious! Now they are so fashionable that magazines run solemn pieces every winter po-facedly advising which boot colours are in this season. You know that you are in Fashion Land when something is described as 'wine stained' as opposed to 'purple' (although here's a hint: unless you're in *The Rocky Horror Picture Show* your boots should never be either). It is stating the obvious somewhat (although this is a fashion book so it would be downright illegal not to at some point) to elaborate on why boots are useful: they're flattering, they're warm and they can be worn to work and to play. The downsides are that they can look totally awful and, somewhat impressively for a piece of footwear, they can make you feel fat.

At some point in the past five years manufacturers decided that the way to make high-heeled boots more fashionable and therefore more desirable was to make them narrower. Clothes designers, it hardly needs stating (although this is a fashion book et cetera and so forth), have been working this wheeze for years because items clearly made for thin people are somehow indicative of how up one's own market (as well as something else) one is. And this is fine, albeit a little morally troubling, were it not for the fact that a lot of customers found they couldn't get the wretched boots on their legs. No longer was just finding the correct size for one's foot the issue, now one had to bear in mind one's calf circumference, too. And for those of us who forget our damn pin number on a weekly basis, this can seem like a numerical demand too far. Meanwhile, because the fashion world tends to work in extremes, others made their boots with mouths as cavernous as the Grand Canyon, all the better to make one's legs look comparatively thinner, my dear. And to let the rain in and soak your ankles and rot the inside of your boots. And to give you absolutely no support at all, probably resulting in a broken ankle. But, hey, at least your legs are lookin' thin, so who cares?

And even once you find a calf-tolerant boot brand there are some rules. Absolutely never with bare legs unless you see the poster for *Pretty Woman* as your own personal *Vogue* magazine, in which case at least ignore that weird way Julia Robert's top was pinned to her skirt – it was very annoying. Never out dancing unless you've always been curious to have empirical evidence of whether your calves have sweat glands.

Boots in any colour other than black, brown and the occasional soft grey are illegal by order of the matter of taste and patterned boots may result in custodial sentencing. Boots operate in a very similar vein to tights in that they should flatter your legs, keep them warm and work with as many garments as possible: to splash them with bright colours and patterns pretty much decimates all of those requisites.

Because boots lengthen the leg automatically, you can get away with quite a small heel, even – gasp! – a kitten heel. For high heels, make sure you go chunky, unless you are still rocking *Pretty Woman* chic, though you might want to ask yourself whether you trust a movie that promotes prostitution as a clever career path for something as important as footwear inspiration.

Biker boots are OK and rather fun to stomp around in and are definitely to be preferred to Ugg-by-name-ugh-by-nature boots. Just don't wear them too literally, i.e. with a biker outfit, but rather with what proper fashion writers call 'a soupçon of contrast', i.e. a posh dress or skirt and top, as opposed to a ripped kilt and safety pins.

Ankle boots are basically the conniving bastard offspring of the boot dynasty, the slightly deformed outsider sneering at the conventional beauty of his distant relatives, and occasionally threatening, but never quite managing, to usurp their dominant hold.

Here is what boots are supposed to do: keep you warm; look smart; provide ease of mobility; be comfortable. Here is what ankle boots do: absolutely none of the above.

There is no denying that, as footwear goes, ankle boots are pretty much up there with wedge-heeled trainers in terms of silliness. They make you look like a member of the cloven hoof species, they are surprisingly hard to walk in due to lack of – despite the name – ankle support and they go with only about two pieces of clothing, namely knee length or above dresses, particularly tunics, and the occasional short skirt, all of which have to be worn with tights, unless you are going for the reality-TV girl-band look.

Trousers with ankle boots will prompt wits to ask if Little Piggy is going to market, particularly if the trousers are cropped or, sweet Jesus, tucked into the boots.

And yet, unlike the aforementioned and deeply upsetting trainers, ankle boots make one come over all Fatboy Slim in wanting to praise them, like we do.

Yes, they look ridiculous. And, yes, your calves will resemble stuffed sausages. However, sometimes a woman just doesn't – gasp! – care if something makes her look like Scarlett Johansson or not (see *Get, fashion that girls do and boys don't*). For a start, ankle boots are a glorious alternative to their more mainstream mother ship, knee-length boots, which are always useful but occasionally just a wee bit dull. Ankle boots, however, suggest that the wearer is no safe, mainstream, probably-a-fan-of-Coldplay kinda lady: oh no, forget about Gwyneth Paltrow, we got Courtney Love over here, gentlemen. And, fine, perhaps Courtney is not every woman's life counsellor but, damn, it would be pretty boring to eat mung beans every day.

And most importantly of all, they are really good fun to dance in. This makes them pretty much unique in the world of female footwear. They may not provide as much support as normal boots, but are more stable than heels and just more of a laugh than flats. Thus, they are one of the few benefits to the near annual eighties fashion revivals, just about compensating for the accompanying jumper dresses (scratchy and surprisingly unflattering) and designer hair scrunchies (elaboration unnecessary) that emerge with them.

As for cowboy boots, well. Although this book is in favour of using clothes to play dress up and have a bit of fun in general, there are some looks which are forbidden unless they are an actual necessity. 'Safari' is definitely up there in regards to all non-jungle based activity, and skirts going by the somewhat un-PC name of 'peasant' should not have their hems dragging along any kind of pavement. But number one is anything dubbed 'cowboy'. Jackets, shirts and, most of all, boots are just about tolerable in a rodeo context, and that's merely out of respect for tradition coupled with gracious tolerance of a people who think standing around a dirt ring watching a man grip on to an angry bull constitutes a good night out. Because they make one's legs look thin and because they are associated with second-hand markets they have become the favoured footwear of posh girls. But, ladies, other things can slim the leg than some overly stitched boot and the reason you always find them in markets is because they are rubbish and their original owners have finally come to their senses and given them away. This latter point, incidentally, can be applied to overly floral dresses, manky old fur and beaten-up satchel bags (see *Vintage*). Men who favour cowboy boots believe that adding a couple of cheeky extra inches in height compensates for resembling some ageing wannabe playboy strolling the beach front in Capri. This assumption is mistaken. If you really do want to hoik up your height, for heaven's sake just slip on an innocuous Chelsea boot, or even a simple brogue with a subtle heel. Unless there truly is a danger of you needing to round up the horses at a moment's notice, there is absolutely no excuse.

And as for pirate boots, the rising wave of despair swamps the necessary flame of outrage, leaving only a wheezing puff of distress.

Cardigans, *a trend in action*

The recent resurrection of the cardigan provides a useful illustration of the inner mechanics of a fashion trend.

Everyone knows the general trajectory: every six months the fashion magazines announce that a previously unthinkable look is just positively de rigeur this season. The public applauds and eagerly flaps credit cards in sales assistants' faces. Six months later the style cognoscenti announce, with untroubled amnesia, that actually that look is hideous and now it's all about some even more unlikely style.

Some say that this is merely the fashion industry's way of making people fork out their money twice a year on goods they heretofore never would have considered. Others claim that six months is the time it takes for the public to realize that their newly favoured look of a tunic top over leggings which once seemed ever so cutting edge was actually sampled then rejected by Debbie Gibson twenty years ago. While both of these theories have a degree of merit, they are unnecessarily cynical. The truth is the public likes new things. So just as the once seemingly insurpassable appeal of Cowgirl Barbie dramatically wanes with the new arrival of Tahiti Barbie in the eyes of a five-year-old girl (and rightly so – the latter has hair down to her ankles), so those tunic dresses are going to lose their lustre after a couple of months to those same girls several years on, thanks to general fatigue caused by over exposure, bad celebrities (see *Celebrities, and when bad ones happen to good fashion*) and, most importantly, the appearance of new clothes in the shops and on glossy magazine covers.

The cardigan is an interesting example, because here is a garment that was sartorial shorthand for mousey frumpishness and yet suddenly became the fash mags' favourite pet; a state of being that lasted for a nigh on unthinkably long period of time (i.e. roughly three seasons).

Not that this has ever prevented something being dubbed a fashion trend, but there are several problems with the cardigan, hence its previous residency in fashion purdah. For a start, it is far fussier than a simple pullover in the way it will always slip off one shoulder and hang in a niggling uneven fashion. Next, no matter how hard the sell made by the fashion dictators, there is no getting away from the fact that a cardigan would make even Serena Williams look a bit girlishly helpless, which not everyone sees as a boon. How very apt it was that the group that sang possibly the most simperingly twee song ever to appear in a half-decent film was called The Cardigans, known pretty much only for the grating song, 'Lovefool', from the otherwise always acceptable *Romeo + Juliet* (points deducted for the stupid plus sign in the title). Finally, the age at which the cardigan slips from making a woman look like a Darling Bud of May to Miss Marple in hot pursuit of a villainous scoundrel is very difficult to ascertain and, because not everyone appreciates the beauty of the latter, many prefer to avoid the garment and the issue altogether.

To be fair, the cardigan wasn't an entirely outlandish garment to bring into the fashion fold. Proudly skinny ladies have long loved them because they keep their undernourished bodies warm in place of any calories to burn internally yet they also are slim fitting, thereby showing off one's jutting shoulder blades and twiggish upper arms a treat, hence their popularity with the likes of Coco Chanel and the ladies-who-don't-lunch. In terms of women's never ending search for a garment that they can wear with a dress or jeans, it made for an understandable follower to the eighties shoulder-padded jacket and nineties sporty hooded top. Designers can get away with making quite expensive versions in cashmere and fiddly beading while the high street can knock out versions made so cheaply you can almost hear the gentle whimpers of sweatshop-bound children emanating from the stitches as you try them on. It fitted in perfectly with the extremely popular Mitford fashion trend in the early half of this decade. This did not, sadly, involve designers advising women to go to prison with their fascist husbands or to join the communist party but rather to buy lots of tweed skirts, floral dresses and, yes, cardigans and generally look like they were on their way to buy a carton of Carnation milk, ration book safely tucked inside their battered leather Mulberry handbag.

But a cardigan is not exactly a garment that puts one in the mood for breaking out the dancing shoes. Nor is it one that inspires much desire – it is a rare woman who gets too excited about buying just one cardigan, never mind four or five. They're quite a useful basic, yes, but unlike jeans, say, or a thin-knit T-shirt, there's only so much a designer can do with them: they can't be shaped to give you the backside of a Californian teenage surfing champion and they can't be cut to give you Elle McPherson's arms. The most a designer can do is just bead on another flower. Whoop de flipping do. Occasionally you'll find either a super long or a cropped one, but these look simply like the last desperate gasps of a garment vainly fighting its way out of the quicksand of ignominy.

Just as the cardigan was beginning to fade away from the womenswear arena the most unexpected development of all in this garment's career took place: the men seized it for themselves. Well, I say the men did, but it was, of course, the menswear designers who did and then tried to push it into the men's hands with a modicum of surprising relative success. This was a clever ploy on the designers' part because, unlike with women, a cardigan was probably not something that a man already owned thereby meaning he would have to – ah ha! – buy one. But the reason he didn't have one before is because the only man in the public eye in modern times who regularly wears a cardigan is Grampa on *The Simpsons* who may well spout the occasional memorable bon mot but does not, to be brutal, sport a look that most young men, or old men, for that matter, desperately wish to emulate.

But that, of course, is precisely the appeal. Because men's fashion still, incredibly, has to fight against weirdly conservative and often frankly homophobic prejudices, the braver souls often react rather like rebellious teenagers, opting for the most extreme and unlikely looks possible. This explains the endless carousel of neon clothes, patterned trousers and other garments so misguided they defy description (although here are three words: Prada angora leggings) that men's style magazines trot out every year. The eternal popularity of geek chic clothing, popularized by labels such as Comme des Garçons, Jil Sander and Prada, is very much part of this as there is something so satisfyingly perverse about the idea of a £700 designer anorak. Plus, seeing as men have yet to be convinced to spend a grand on a handbag in the way that women have, they have to communicate their level of fashion awareness to fellow members of the in crowd with the clothes and surely nothing says fashion in-ness better than a designer men's cardigan.

This does mean that the cardigan is a little more niche in the men's sector than it is in the women's. But at least this gave the cardigan an extended life and confirmed to designers that they might be able to conserve their precious brain cells and earn a few extra bucks simply by transferring clothes on the wane in the women's sector over to the men's, just as they had already discovered with skinny jeans. Best of all, it made a style icon out of a man who once perceptively proclaimed that the metric system was the tool of the devil.

Celebrities, and when bad ones happen to good fashion

*R*arely has the phrase 'making a deal with the devil' been more accurate than when describing the fashion world's alignment with celebrities. The appeal was always obvious and inevitable: a photo of Sarah Jessica Parker swinging around a Dior saddle bag gets far more press attention and ensuing sales than when it is carried by some unknown model on a catwalk. And you don't even have to convince the celebrities to wear anything: not long ago designers realized that just plopping some random TV stars into the front row of a show guarantees the designer's name appearing in that week's issue of *Now!/New!/Wow!/Who?* magazine that week, an ambition Cristóbal Balenciaga tragically died too early to achieve himself and, late at night, you can almost hear his spirit sobbing from beyond in regret.

With convenient synchronicity, celebrities realized that carrying the latest £1,500 bag got them extra magazine coverage, seeing as such shots proved an easy way for magazine editors to appease those pesky advertisers. Even more excitingly, some clever celebrities realized they could actually make a whole career out of this wheeze, with absolutely no particular ones coming libellously to mind.

But because magazines propagated the idea that carrying a really expensive bag or wearing the latest Prada dress was somehow proof of the celebrity's inherent superiority over the rest of the world, as opposed to just being proof that they have a stylist, other celebrities from slightly further down the food chain began to get in on the act and this is when things became a tad more interesting.

Fashion is about image, from Dolce & Gabbana's molto sexy mentality versus Marc Jacobs's aura of downtown cool, and it is this image that nudges customers to choose one over the other, depending on their ideal self-fantasy. The clothes are actually almost irrelevant – it is created pretty much entirely by advertising and celebrity association. For example, J-Lo goes to a Dolce show, whereas Sofia Coppola is Marc Jacobs's front-row friend. So there is nothing like a celebrity at odds with the designer's carefully cultivated image daring to wear something from the collection to show just how fragile this system is and how utterly irrelevant it is to the general customer.

Thus, the Z-lister simultaneously becomes both the naked emperor as well as the wise little boy shouting about the nudity, giving an unexpectedly almost metaphysical element to a photo of, say, Alex Curran wearing a Prada dress.

A classic example of this was when Rebecca Loos, at the height of her lofty career, wore a Temperley dress to a film première. Now, Temperley is a brand, more explicitly than most, which has concentrated on building an image, in this case, one of a bucolic, English society lifestyle in which one's greatest stress is to get out of the Notting Hill traffic on a Friday night in order to get to Mummy and Daddy's farm in Shropshire before Cook serves supper.

On the plus side it was rare that the word 'Temperley' had ever appeared in the British tabloids before that fated day, so perhaps designer Alice Temperley can console herself thinking about the extra publicity. However, it is unlikely that a woman who described how she was once having text message sex with a certain footballer in a museum and had to 'finish myself off in the loo' was quite the customer Alice envisaged skipping about in her beaded minidresses. Getting on to Victoria Newton's Bizarre page in the *Sun* probably doesn't give designers the same kind of thrill as being worn by Sienna Miller on the cover of *Vogue*.

And for this reason, Z-list celebrities are the fashion customer's greatest friends. They show the reality of what the clothes are like, away from the image nonsense and prove that, while Cate Blanchett might look all glamorous and glacial, this has nothing to do with the dress she is wearing, it's because she is, duh, glamorous and glacial. Z-listers are the fashion litmus test because the clothes have to be not only good enough to look nice on normal women, but to be so good that they can overcome the negative Z-lister association and, really, you shouldn't spend designer-level money on anything that offers less. For example, a certain ruffled Chloé skirt still retained its appeal after being worn by Coleen, proving that it earned its £600 price tag because it was genuinely very pretty, but many other garments have been duly swept away.

The most interesting example of celebrities destroying fashion items is that of Heather Mills, McCartney as was. The day after it was announced that this heartless woman was daring to get divorced from Saint Paul she was photographed wearing pretty much head-to-toe clothes from what looked remarkably like her soon-to-be-former step-daughter's collection, including, most noticeably, over-the-knee boots, a look Stella had rather bravely been pushing for years. Some were confused as to Heather's motives here: was she showing that, despite the increasingly acrimonious divorce, she was still a family woman, even if that family looked like they wanted to take out an undercover hitman on her? Was she sending out an unlikely olive branch to Stella? Were the boots an ironic comment on the call-girl accusations with which she had been lobbed? Was she just so damn cheap that despite having access to wealth that would rival that of most African countries, she only wore clothes that she was presumably given for free? Or was it that she knew photographs of her wearing those clothes would cause far more damage to Stella than anything she could ever say in court? Frankly, it's almost enough to make you admire the woman.

Classics *with a twist*

*R*hetorical questions are so annoying, aren't they? Nevertheless, it has to be asked, has this formula ever worked for anything?

A common irritant is boyish clothes that have been 'girlified', such as dresses made from elongated hoodies or high-heeled trainers, spawn of the devil if there ever was one. Kinda sassy but still girlish in a Rizzo from *Grease* way, is the intended message; very annoying and wincingly pointless is the obvious result.

With the exception of shorts, some miniskirts and the occasional jacket, denim should only be used for jeans. There is something so inanely gimmicky about dresses, long skirts and trench coats made out of denim. 'Yes, yes, well done,' one longs to say to the wearer of a denim coat, perhaps with a consoling if not exactly sympathetic pat on the arm. 'You've taken a fabric usually used on trousers and used it for, yes, something else. Amazing.'

A dress with a pattern usually reserved for home furnishings won't look like you are making a cheeky nod to the brilliance of design in general; it will make you look like a coffee table. And let's not even get started on three-quarter-length trousers and miniskirts with combat-trouser-style side pockets – cropped trousers and miniskirts being well-known garb for warfare. Obviously, wearing, say, plain black trousers and polo necks is unremittingly boring, but a hee-hawing fashion gimmick is the sartorial equivalent of an embarrassing uncle doing a joke routine coined during the Crusades in front of your friends and then punching them on the shoulder to ask if they got it.

Cleavage, *and the plumbing of depths*

*S*how me a woman with a good three inches of cleavage on show and I'll show you a woman who has little faith in her powers of conversation. All fashion is, to a degree, some form of self-expression in that it gives onlookers an impression of your personality before you open your mouth. Some style choices, however, are there purely to head off the need to open one's mouth at all simply because they come with such an immutable set of associations and assumptions. Animal print is one such example (see *Animal print, when women roar*). Doc Martin boots on women is another (message: MAKE ASSUMPTIONS ABOUT MY SEXUALITY AND I'LL KICK YOU IN THE HEAD!). Cleavage takes this to a whole new level because not only does it mitigate the need for conversation, but any conversation attempted will be rendered pointless anyway as no one will be listening to it, either because they're (a) straight males and therefore rendered temporarily hypnotized, a cliché, yes, but sad and true, or (b) anyone else and are thus left shocked by the pathetic obviousness of your tactics. All women know this. Thus, to get 'em out like this suggests that you believe you have nothing else to offer in the conversation stakes and are compensating accordingly. There's nothing wrong with a woman embracing her sexual power, but when she hoiks it up under everyone's noses with the desperation of a drunken auntie seizing the mike at the end of her nephew's bar'mitzvah for a quick rendition of Chakha Khan, protests must be made.

Yes, you have breasts – congratulations. Whether squashing them together like two pigs fighting underneath a blanket shows them off to their best advantage is a somewhat debatable point. Whether it adds anything to your outfit is less so because the answer is, no, it doesn't. This is not to say you should button it up to Mother Superior levels but, as Maria discovered in *The Sound of Music*, just a slight loosening of the habit is far more effective than a full-on vamp look, something the Baroness found out too late and to her misfortune.

Just as you shouldn't spill out your life story on the first date (another frequent female mistake), so you shouldn't offer up the whole feast to the initial onlooker. After all, you want to be able to offer something later, don't you?

To some women, getting out the cleavage is a Pavlovian response to the prospect of a big night out: they simply don't feel in the party mood unless they can keep hold of a couple of twenties and probably their mobile phone without the assistance of a handbag. But a big night out is precisely when you should tuck it away, simply because the potential for, as Janet Jackson would probably put it, 'wardrobe malfunctions' is that much greater. So unless you want to look like Meg Mathews in her nineties glory days, button up.

A subtle V-neck is fine; a hint of more to come, courtesy of a wrap dress, grand; a full-on navel-plunging affair, unless you're in the Ziegfield Follies, no. And anyway, do you really want to talk to men's flaking bald spots all night? Do you really think you have nothing more to offer than two pillows of fat squished together? And do you really want to attract the attentions of those men who are so easily hypnotized? Come on, girlfriend, raise the bar a little. True, Elizabeth Hurley made a career out of a cleavage-baring dress, but hers is a career some of us have never fully grasped anyway.

Clutch 'bag'

*W*ith the notable exception of buttons and zips, always be wary of something that is named after what it does. If the item in question was of any good use whatsoever, someone would have bothered to give it a proper name instead of just calling it by its verb. To whit, all a fly does is fly and you can't do anything with a peel but peel it. The clutch confirms the truth of this age-old adage and if you need further proof of this accessory's utter redundancy, the verb is not even a particularly nice one. Clutching on for dear life, clutching straws – all perfectly acceptable sentences, yes, but hardly ones redolent of aspirational glamour or, in fact, any positive qualities at all.

The clutch has somehow managed to lay claim to being a member of the bag family despite failing to fulfil what most would consider to be the two most basic requirements of a bag: you cannot fit anything in it and it is a complete pain to carry around.

This issue of bags at parties is utterly tedious because of the gaping canyon between pretty and practical. But a bag the size of a cheque book really won't help anyone strike a balance across that lacuna. With its faux suggestions of vintageness and its lack of strap, thereby not detracting from your exciting bare shoulder action, the clutch has, with its wily, um, clutches, convinced female wedding guests around the world that it is the bag de soirée du choix. But look, at a party you actually do need to carry around quite a bit because aside from the usual phone-keys-purse nexus you will in all likelihood want to chuck in some make-up and maybe a compact for occasional teeth observation, absolutely none of which will fit into your clutch and you'll find yourself actually wasting brain cells before the party by considering phrases like 'Shall I sacrifice the crème blush for the lip gloss?' and 'Maybe if I take the fags out of the box they'll take up less room' (they will, but they'll all get crushed and you'll never fully get all those flakes of dried nicotine out of the lining). Even more annoying is that you have to carry the stupid, bulging thing around all night, like a cat presenting a freshly killed baby robin.

The whole point of a bag is to liberate your hands for important things like drinks, cigarettes, canapés and flirtatious hand brushing. With the clutch, because you will only have one free hand, you end up having to do what is known in medical circles as the Party Multi Finger Splay, holding the neck of your glass between your little and ring fingers, your phone between your ring and middle fingers and your cigarette between your fore and middle fingers which, as you light it, results in you spilling your drink down your cleavage.

And because you have to carry the clutch, you are guaranteed to leave it somewhere in your over-exuberant party state, most probably under your chair or, that well-known black hole of ladies' accessories, on top of a toilet cistern.

So if you don't feel like ending the party in a drunken hysterical state, trying to find the damn clutch by calling your phone, only to be too drunk to remember your number, just purchase a respectable-sized smart bag with a pretty strap. Honestly, there is not a man in this land who has ever thought, 'Yeah, I'd have taken her number, but she had this really annoying bag swinging around her shoulders,' and if there is, well, thank your prudent stars you were saved from any further encounters with such an accessories tyrant.

Coats, *stuck at the nexus point between dull and stressful*

*U*nder normal circumstances, few things please the human species more than an accepted excuse to spend a lot of money on a single piece of indulgence. Hence the otherwise incomprehensible enthusiasm among certain men for five-figure-priced watches (it's, like, science and art in one, yeah?) and pretty much the entire home technology market (you watch TV every day, right? So might as well make it a flat-screen high-def one and don't spare the bank account!).

Like bags and shoes, coats fall under this umbrella in that they are to be worn every day, need to be made relatively well to withstand the elements and have to work with a wide variety of outfits. Yet because they lack that crucial toy element that accessories have they simply do not spark the same excitement. Moreover, coats do not carry the tannoy message of designer status like bags do, most coats not being laden down with gold chains and garish patterns (and we'll return to the problem of those that are), so they don't even have the mitigating appeal of flash factor. Instead, one is left standing in the department or high-street store coat section, whirling around in a sea of rails of black and grey woollen winterwear, freighted down with mental lists of practical requirements for a coat, already wearied by the prospect of having to find something that you can bear to wear every day and, frankly, quite tempted to say bugger it to the whole enterprise and go to the in-store cafeteria for a watery cappuccino and a quick flick through *Grazia*.

But limpid caffeinated drinks will keep a lady warm for only so long so it's back to the coat issue.

Obviously, the ideal would be to have as many coats as possible, maybe even a different one for each outfit. But not all of us can be the Queen, and even Barbara Amiel, it transpired, wasn't able to maintain the Barbara Amiel lifestyle without help, so you need a coat that works with the probable two basics in your wardrobe: smart work skirts and jeans.

Princess coats – knee-length coats with a double row of buttons down the front, usually with a nipped in high waist and a small collar – have proven surprisingly adept in this department in that they look pretty with dresses and skirts and are a fast route to feminizing your Saturday-afternoon hangover outfit of jeans and trainers. Unfortunately, they can make one look like one is wearing Bonpoint for adults.

For want of a better description, the recently popular pouffed coats – like princess coats but with the bottom half puffing gently outwards in an almost oval shape – work better in this respect just because they look more cleverly made and thus a little less Playskool.

Trench coats, too, work with skirts and jeans but they fail to fulfill pretty much every other requirement of a coat and are thus to be treated with sceptical caution (see *Trench coats*).

Similarly, because you need to wear your coat not just often but in multiple scenarios, don't get a patterned one. Aside from the fact that you will be so sick to the back of your teeth by the pattern come February that your fillings actually vibrate every time you look at it (see *Patterns – or test patterns?*), you won't be able to wear your coat with half your wardrobe – i.e. your patterned half – without resembling a human acid trip. Moreover, there is something a little too deliberately wacky about the patterned coat, particularly winter ones, in their determined desire to announce one's cheerful nature to all and sundry. To be confronted with a red-and-pink striped coat

speckled with polka dots on the train home from work on a January evening is akin to being seized by the lapels by a gurning fool who shrieks in your face that eternally helpful observation to 'cheer up, it might never happen'.

Military-style coats can have a similarly wearing effect as patterned ones on anyone who isn't actually in the military. Plus they can make one resemble the model of a modern major general in a local Gilbert & Sullivan revival, a Pete Doherty obsessed saddo or a Chelsea Pensioner. Such negatives aside, the military coat does actually improve many outfits. Just as a recalcitrant young scallywag will be whipped into shape by a sharp tongued corporal (editorial clarification to reader: all knowledge regarding the military in this book comes from *An Officer and a Gentleman* and *A Few Good Men*), so a strict military jacket pulls together a similarly sloppy outfit, particularly the aforementioned hangover jeans uniform. Military coats often have belts, which is another plus because too many winter coats make one look even more shapeless and lumpen than one tends to feel in the British wintertime anyway. For this reason, A-line coats – occasionally called swing or trapeze cuts, presumably in an attempt to add a bit of all too rare circus fun to the subject of winter outerwear – can appeal in their pleasing ability to disguise entirely a body bloated out with hearty food and winter inertia. However, you will be asked by uncomprehending male friends at least once a day whether you are pregnant and this assuredly does not help a lady's Seasonal Affective Disorder a jot.

Full-length coats might provide the bodily coverage factor with an added dose of drama, but sweep down the street in one on a dark winter's night and you will petrify onlookers, convinced they are witnessing the resurrection of Jack the Ripper.

Puffa jackets are the comfort food of the winter clothing world: their effect on your physical appearance is rarely beneficial, but they are what you retreat to when in that mood known to psychologists as 'not giving a stuff'. For that reason, the reader is advised to own at least one of the above, even if the puffa will make you look like Kenny from *South Park*. The parka, meanwhile, comes in probably the only shade on the planet that doesn't look good on a single skin tone, but it allows you to keep wearing your summer dresses in the winter, now worn with woolly tights, and, most importantly, will make you feel like you're walking around in a giant duvet. And, if we're being wholly honest here, that is pretty much what you're looking for from a coat in the first place.

Dates, *and why they are the one event you really needn't worry about what you wear*

*T*here are many movies out there that contain essential human truths, but few that have been better encapsulated than in a single line of dialogue from *Clueless*. No, not the bit when Cher announces to her father that her day's achievement was that she 'broke in my purple clogs' (although that can come in useful sometimes), but the moment when her quarry Christian leaves their video date abruptly, destroying her dreams of shucking off her unwanted virginity. 'What's wrong with me?' she wails internally, throwing herself against the closing front door. 'Did my hair go flat?' David O. Selznick died without ever helping to realize such a true piece of dialogue.

Of course, as all readers know, hair flatness was the least of the issues here. The fact that Christian was, in fact, gay may help to make this situation even more tragically familiar to female fashion followers. The point is, while Cher was fussing over the minutiae, Christian was looking at a much bigger picture – namely, that she was the wrong gender – and it was a picture Cher hadn't even thought to envisage.

Of course you want to look nice for your date. But you know what looks best of all? You feeling comfortable, relaxed and confident that you look good (and being the right sex). Yes, yes, this does all sound a bit cheerleaderish and fist-in-the-air, but, honestly, you could find the shortest, slinkiest, sexiest dress in the world, but if you spend the whole evening tugging at your cleavage and pulling down the hem you might as well have worn a burlap flipping sack for all the seduction you're pulling there. So don't wear any stupid shoes you can't walk in and don't wear anything that will give you hypothermia; just stick with an old favourite that always makes you feel good and has garnered you compliments in the past. Honestly, he really, really doesn't mind if he's seen it before. Most boys don't notice that kind of thing and, if they do, they don't care because they have no idea how many more dresses you have squashed away at the back of your cupboard so won't wonder why you keep pulling on the same LBD. Anyway, they only have two jackets so who are they to judge?

Generally, when it comes to women's outfits, men take a Coldplay approach: if the overall melody is good, it doesn't matter if the individual components or lyrics don't make the slightest dash of sense. A girl laughing and dancing and making sparkly conversation = attractive; a girl whinging about being cold and insisting on getting a taxi for a 200-yard distance = a colossal pain.

Most guys are pretty mainstream and don't, really, want their girlfriends to look like the kinda lady their friends could easily have as soon as their back is turned, and if they do want this, you may want to check their passport to see if the listed occupation is 'pimp'.

Here is what boys like: well-fitted skinny or bootcut jeans with a nice top, T-shirt or V-neck jumper, maybe with boots over the jeans but ideally just some little heels or flats; a simple dress that nips in around your waist but is otherwise loose and feminine with (and you will begin to see a recurring theme in this list) a-bit-of-a-V-neck;

a quite body-fitted dress that is compensated by being of a modest length, i.e. knee length or just above – with a-bit-of-a-V-neck; a denim miniskirt with little heels or flats and a pretty (possibly beaded, possibly plain) top with a-bit-of-a-V-neck. Beginning to see the general point here, aren't you: something pretty but unthreatening, something they could take home to meet their parents but is still quite blatantly fanciable, something that is relatively modest but still suggests the possibility of a feminine body beneath and these are all, as happy chance would have it, things that most women feel comfortable wearing. Yes, we are talking the sartorial embodiment of Cat Deeley. Or think of it this way: it's like leading a donkey to drink – you entice him on with a trustworthy wholesome nature but dangle a little bit of a carrot in front of his downy nose, hinting that there may be some more joys to come other than just water.

Meeting up with your girlfriends is actually a far more stressful fashion occasion because they will notice the individual pieces, they will know what kind of look you're attempting here and because none of them, presumably, will be mentally occupied by wondering whether they'll get a snog out of this, you won't be able to distract them from your clothes with your fantastic body and gorgeous face. Hopefully, though, because they are your friends, they will take a tolerant attitude to any errors. If not, you may want to reconsider your wardrobe, not to mention your social circle.

Decade rehashing *and why designers live in the past*

*G*osh, it's exciting to work in fashion! Every season, one boards the Tardis and emerges in a different time period! Wow! One year, we're all 'very fifties', the next 'it's all gone seventies' (this, it must be reiterated for emphasis, is obviously a reference to decades, not, heavens forfend, age).

Partly, this is just a sign of laziness on the part of fashion journalists and designers. To the former, this kind of decade rehashing is just a sloppy, and often historically inaccurate, shorthand for describing clothes when one's mental thesaurus runs dry. Hence, a dress with a tight waist is a sign that one has entered the fifties; the presence of a long skirt and floppy hat is a stronger indication than the disillusionment with the incumbent Labour government that we're back in the late seventies. Well, there are only so many times a person can write 'high waisted' or 'long hems' before eating one's elbow out of boredom.

To be fair to the journalists, designers are extremely fond of rolling back the years. Sixties shift dresses, eighties jumper dresses, seventies long dresses – all have been resurrected in modern times and it is a rare year that doesn't have what is known in professional circles as 'a bit of a flares moment'. Some stand and cheer this touching sign of respect for the past by designers; everyone else, particularly those who lived through the decade being resurrected, cups their ears and hears the screech of a barrel scrape.

If, as is frequently claimed in those boring articles justifying 'the point of fashion' or 'the relevance of couture', a designer's job is to show us new ways to dress and, ergo, see ourselves, then wheeling out a bunch of minidresses, the subtle mechanics of which Twiggy instructed us in forty years ago, does indicate that someone, somewhere is falling down on the job. Possibly into a pile of cocaine in a nightclub in Soho, thereby stripping the brain of the cells making up the 'originality' part of cerebral functions.

Moreover, there is something rather selfish about relying so heavily on the past. After all, what looks will we leave for our future descendents to copy? What on earth will TV bosses of the future be able to use to illustrate their programmes? What, in short, will be our legacy? Hipster jeans? The thong? Ugg boots? Coinages to be proud of, one and all, and not, one could add, born from the catwalks. So remind me again, what is the point of fashion?

On the other hand, the only time this decade revival schtick doesn't work is when something that is blatantly wrong is revived – flares, for example, spring eagerly to the mind. Otherwise, why shouldn't a nice flapper dress (twenties!) or cute tweed jacket (forties!) be sported about town? It seems a little unjust that those born in the seventies, eighties and nineties never get the chance to wear clothes with any form of structure due purely to the misfortune of growing up in such a formless era.

If people can po-facedly claim that the Grace Kelly or Angie Bowie are this season's hottest trends then wheeling out a time period doesn't seem that unreasonable. After all, fashion is literally just about dressing up. Kit yourself up like a late member of a minor European royal family, or go for generic hippy – six of one, half a dozen of the other, really.

And, anyway, let's be a little sympathetic to the designers because it's not as if everyone doesn't idealize the past, in particular, the past of their childhood. This explains the current eighties fashion revival because quite a few of the more popular designers today (Stella McCartney, Nicolas Ghesquière at Balenciaga) were kids in the eighties. It is a hard-proven fact that the most formative outfit in anyone's life is what your teenage babysitter wore when you were a child. My God, did anything ever look so cool as what your sixteen-year-old neighbour wore when your parents were out and sat on your sofa and talked on the phone to her boyfriend for three hours? Really, if designers seriously wanted to flog clothes faster they should just get rid of the wan-faced models and hire a bunch of gum-chewing spotty teenagers toting around their GCSE coursework to walk the runways. Nothing like a Proustian moment to sell some ankle boots as is proven by the fact that customers love this decade rehashing as much as designers do. If they didn't, the designers wouldn't do it. Pity the screaming barrel.

Dresses, *God's gift to women*

*Y*es, yes, we all know the theory that women wearing trousers in the early twentieth century helped to liberate them from the shackles of male tyranny, et cetera and so forth. But while this may have been a satisfying if symbolic triumph, one can't help but suspect that the words pyrrhic and victory are more apt in this instance. For a start, liberate them to do what? Being able to dance the can can without flashing their knickers? Climb a tree? Like, um, thanks.

Briefly, there is no garment more liberating to women than a dress. Except maybe a nice big hotel bathrobe, but we're not allowed to go to work in those yet. A good dress will never make you feel fat, it can be worn with flats or heels and everybody can find a style that suits them – absolutely none of these statements can be applied to trousers with 100 per cent certainty. I concede that some of the whaleboned dresses our grandmothers were fighting against in days of yore might have left a little to be desired on the comfort front but I haven't seen even a splinter of Moby Dick in Topshop or Zara recently, so I think it's safe to say we've left behind that millstone.

Trousers squeeze round your waist, they squeeze round your thighs, they often make your bum look the size of Ecuador and they slip down ever so immodestly when you sit, and, yes, I am including sainted jeans in all of these criticisms. Dresses do none of the above. With some judicious layering you can wear a summer dress all year round, something you certainly cannot say about summer trousers, and the fact that you only need to deal with one garment in the morning is just the sartorial icing on this fashion gateau.

Just as there is the old rule about the higher the hemline, the lower the heel, so there is a similar theory that says the higher the hemline the longer the sleeves, merely to compensate in terms of flesh coverage. This isn't failsafe, but long sleeves will make you feel a little less of a cliché than a minidress with spaghetti straps even if, to the male onlooker, the effect is pretty much the same, i.e. you're getting your thighs out. If you are going to go for a long-sleeved minidress look, keep the dress fairly loose, like a tunic, unless your chosen Halloween costume this year is that of a Robert Palmer backing singer.

One dress style that does need to be taken to task is the wrap. Much has been written by more manicured hands than my own about how brilliant this style is, how it (again, apparently) 'liberated' women, how it suits everyone, and so on and so on. Well, when anything is deemed to suit 'everyone', you can pretty much disregard all the ensuing guff because that is clearly a load of rubbish (see also *Trench coats*). Nothing suits everyone, and wrap dresses definitely don't. If you have a curvy bust, a narrow waist and a flattish stomach, well done, you have found your uniform. If you fall short in any of those departments, come and take a pew over on this side of the room. Its much praised jersey fabric manages to be both unflatteringly clingy and immodestly loose, an impressive combination only bettered by Jonathan Ross's interviewing technique of being simultaneously greasily sycophantic and painfully crude. And, finally, when the wind blows, well, suffice to say you might be a little more liberated than expected. Whereas the joy of most dresses lies in their kindness to most body types or, at least, their ability to sculpt most body types into a flattering shape, the wrap is kind only to the chosen few and, if your body doesn't confirm, it scoldingly emphasizes its alleged faults.

But wraps aside, dresses are the business and they almost make up for childbirth, periods and bad hair days. Pretty much in that order, in fact.

Drugs, *the role thereof*

'**W**hatever you said about [cocaine],' muses the society maven in Edward St Aubyn's novella *Bad News*, 'it wasn't fattening.' Actually, fashion people could say a lot more about it, and they often do, but then, it's amazing just how chatty two grams before midnight makes you.

Drugs are probably no more popular in the fashion world than they are in the City, the acting or the music industries. Yet because the fashion industry's image fits so nicely with so many of the clichés about drugs – the shallow glitziness, the surplus of cash, not eating for three days at a time, the general talking of bollocks – it is now taken as a general assumption that if you work in fashion your septum must be just about hanging on in there even if you are just the cupboard assistant and barely earn enough in a month to buy a bottle of Day Nurse.

There is no question that drugs are prevalent in fashion, pretty much for all of the reasons above. Heck, you'd really hope they are anyway: the thought that some of the things that people come out with in this business, either in the clothes they design or the arrogant hyperbole they say, are created in the cold light of sobriety is highly disturbing, to say the least.

There is something about making a career out of what you did as a teenager – in this instance, going shopping and admiring yourself in the mirror – that does arguably arrest one's development, as many a rock star has proven in their time. Thus, there remains an attitude, particularly in the fashion world, that getting hold of some drugs is proof of one's inherent coolness even though any schlub with a spare £50 and access to a street corner could pull off that masterstroke.

Anyway, the whole set-up of the fashion industry today pretty much requires a constant supply of ready drugs. For a start, this is a business built on image. Before walking down the catwalk of a show, designers often put up little billboards backstage telling the models to look like fabulous, self-confident sex goddesses, even if it's 9 a.m. on a rainy morning in Milan and the models are all homesick, mal-nourished Russian sixteen-year-olds. 'You are gorgeous and every man wants to fuck you!!!' a designer scrawled one season before his 11 a.m. show, which would probably drive most women either to a pile of drugs to keep from laughing in his face, or else screaming out the back door.

Even if he is on the verge of bankruptcy a designer has to main-tain an attitude of total confidence to give the brand its requisite aspirational desirability. Thus he has to say things like, 'Oh, you should have seen Jade and Kate on the nudist beach in Ibiza – it was just a riot', without throwing up his internal organs in self-disgust.

The PRs need something to cope with the pain of devoting their lives to promoting the work of some screeching nobody with a per-sonality disorder and being treated with, alternately, contempt and sycophancy by journalists, depending on whether their designer is having 'a moment' or not.

Fashion journalists work in both fashion and the media so if they somehow manage to avoid drugs in their career they probably aren't working very much.

The fashion industry is about generating excitement over things like handbags and pretending that you feel fabulous even if you're broke and haven't eaten since Wednesday or slept since Monday. Drugs are very useful for all of these. Moreover, in the fashion world everyone is constantly on show. It is not beyond the realms of pos-sibility that the only reason the antiquated system of fashion shows still exists is so that all the models, designers, PRs and journalists get to spend four weeks together checking out not the clothes but each other (see *Fashion shows, Darwin in action*). Cocaine may well have been created for moments such as these, helping to keep one's chin up, if nose down, when you see Anna Wintour clocking that you are in the eighth row.

Obviously, not everyone in fashion takes drugs. This is, although it is often forgotten, a billion-dollar business, which does suggest that someone out there is working on a Monday morning and not still monged out on Saturday night's ketamine binge. And as some ageing designers have thoughtfully proven to the new generation, the sight of a sixty-five-year-old snorting coke, chuffing down sixty fags a day and burbling about the good old days when people knew how to show respect might well give him a certain image but not perhaps the kind of one that sells handbags.

Anyway, drugs are terribly bad for one's skin and buying them is just short-sighted. Why spend a couple of hundred on some white powder that will be gone by the morning when you can spend the same on a pair of Prada wedges that will last at least three months? You see, not everyone in the business is superficial.

Espadrilles, *the straw dogs that are*

*T*he British man on holiday has never been a particularly edifying sight, but the British man's feet on holiday are worse. Whereas women, of course, have the smooth, perfect feet of carved angels, men's look like they belong to the lead character of *Harry and the Hendersons*. Gnarled and yellowed, cracked and bumpy, a man's foot is not an erotic sight and one doubts if even Fergie would ever want to suck on one, no matter how much reciprocation she owed. There is nothing like seeing some hairy toes to serve as a humbling reminder of our beastly origins.

Most men's summer shoes show off the said protrusions to their full, not exactly blossoming effect, not least the flip flop, the G-string of the footwear world. But with its cheap cheerfulness, there is something rather endearing in the honesty of a flip flop, not least in its acceptance that the only way to dress on holiday is basically to wear what you wore when you used to go on holiday with your parents as a child: knee-length shorts, loose T-shirts, some form of hat that has no American sporting associations and a pair of plastic shoes.

Espadrilles, however, are deceptively pretentious, with their aspirations for continental sophistication due to their vague evocations of orange-skinned Italian playboys strolling along the Capri coast, looking for a few belle ragazze to grab their balls at, those lucky, lucky ladies.

More pressingly, they are completely useless. Simply, it is a little noted fact that on holiday one's feet are always wet, from the ocean, the scummy pool or sweat. Shoes made out of a bit of cotton stretched over some mini blocks of hay really are never been going to be much cop in the face of moistness. In point of fact, they will reek – no, not like freshly mown hay evoking images of idyllic childhood summers, but of mildewed grass and yeasty toes.

True, espadrilles don't have the flip flop's toe-rub downside, but they fall apart faster and, with their tendency towards garish patterns, play to British men's worst style weaknesses. 'Flip flop' is not the most thrillingly of masculine words to say, but it is a damn sight sexier than the scent of rotting straw blowing on the summer breeze.

Ethnic *clothes*

Wonderfully useful word, 'ethnic'. India, China, Thailand, Pago Pago – you name it, they're ethnic, which basically means 'not Britain, America, Australia and maybe France'. In other words, it's not all that dissimilar to Alf Garnett's description of anything beyond his sofa as 'a bit foreign', but with an added dose of faux hippy smugness.

From food to fashion, home décor to varieties of incense, if it looks a bit, well, foreign, and maybe smells a bit funny, it can be described as 'ethnic'.

Ethnic fashion is usually defined by an abundance of cheese-cloth, superfluous embroidery and, if you're really going for it, gold trim. It tends to be particularly popular in delightfully pretty areas of town populated by large well-appointed houses, three wheeled buggies and gourmet delicatessens where one can find the most fabulous quinoa salad for just £7.50 a box. Funnily enough, the one thing you can hardly ever find in these parts of town is any actual 'ethnic' people, save those who clean the aforementioned supersized abodes. Well, maybe the clothes are there to compensate for their absence, like in pagan cultures when dolls are dressed in the clothes of the dead to honour their absence.

Appreciating other cultures is always to be recommended. And certainly there are many aspects to eastern-style dress that one cannot but appreciate: it's often very pretty, British ladies tend to be instinctively drawn to floaty fabrics and, unless you've bought a belly dancer's costume, it generally gives good coverage.

The problem with this kind of fashion tourism is its underlying insinuations, which are generally about as subtle as a hot pink kaftan top trimmed with little bells around the cuffs.

There are three types of people who favour what they would describe as 'the ethnic look': the liberal upper-middle classes, self-congratulatory travellers and yoga teachers. All three use the clothes to send out the same message: namely, I am deeply spiritual, me, far above you with your west-o-centric high-street lifestyle. Not so far above, mind, that I can resist shoving this belief in your face via my paisley kaftan. Shanti shanti.

I'm glad you had such an epiphanically life-changing experience in Jaipur / Marrakech / Ibiza – no, really, I am. But just as no one wants to hear other people's holiday anecdotes, sporting head to toe ethnic clothing is not very far off from wearing your holiday pictures safety-pinned about your person, and about as interesting. A small touch here and there – dangly silver earrings, say, or a floaty top with a pair of denim shorts, or some pretty flip flops – fine;

going for the full-on sequined Gandhi look when popping down to the organic market verges on becoming offensive fancy dress. If we even get started on white people with dreadlocks then this book will, I fear, descend into full-on expletives, but, two words: sunburned scalp. You're feeling the spiritualism now, aren't you?

Anyway, I'm not all that sure if buying some embroidered tops from a boutique in Hampstead which itself bought them cheap as chips from a stallholder in Pushkar and then slapped on a 1,500 per cent mark-up is necessarily the best sign of one's deep affinity for another culture. Tempting as it is to suggest that the £175 for a pastel beach kaftan might be better spent on a charity for that country, one doesn't want to be as smug as the ethnic look-ers so, with a pained sigh, let's just draw the curtain.

Exercise clothes, *the new couture*

This is a true story: due to a clerical error I once stayed at a ridiculously fashionable hotel in Beverly Hills. Mindful of taking full advantage of this most unfortunate state of affairs I sauntered on down to the pool in my favourite plain blue bikini, a pair of simple black shorts, some flip flops and ordered some breakfast. From my fellow guests' reaction to me, you'd have thought that Mrs Shrek had taken up residence, pool side. My first mistake was that despite being female I had ordered food. The other mistakes were almost as shameful: first, my bathing suit was notably lacking in Versace gold chains, Gucci military detailing (think Halle Berry in James Bond), Missoni tassels and other similar detailing that generally suggest one is more interested in letting others know that you spent over £200 on a bathing suit than any actual swimming. And what was I thinking, going for French Connection shorts instead of a designer sarong, a.k.a a long scarf that falls off every time you try to stand up due to scarves generally being made to go around one's neck, not one's waist? That I had neglected to put on make-up – yes, make-up, at 10 a.m., to, lest we forget, lie by the pool – was almost incidental.

Fine, this is a fairly extreme example, as examples from LA tend to be. But it is merely a magnification of a general truth: ever since the eighties when exercise became fashionable, it was inevitable that its accoutrements and uniform would have to follow suit.

Go to any yoga class and marvel at the predominance of cute little vest tops decorated with lotus flowers by Christy Turlington's Nuala label and sexily low-slung velour trousers. There are even trends regarding yoga mats (pink is very passé; it's all about natural fibres now, or at least Stella McCartney's dusty rose version for Adidas), just as the Indian yogis always hoped for. Go to a gym and delight in all the increasingly technical trainers that look like they were invented to assist the wearer to fly to the moon without the aid of NASA as opposed to completing thirty minutes on the step machine. Inevitably, it is the trendiest sports – surfing, skiing and yoga – that have the strictest and snobbiest rules regarding fashion, with every year throwing up new rubric. The 'what to wear on the slopes' is now an annual staple in fashion magazines.

On one level, I cannot but applaud this trend towards making any actual exercise irrelevant. And there is something very pleasing about the idea of self-described gym fans shopping for ever more expensive exercise outfits as procrastination to avoid getting on the treadmill. Well done, Oh athletic ones – so glad you have come round to the general view at last.

But after seeing one too many photos of Kate Moss

on the slopes with her baby daughter, the former in a giant fur hat, the latter in Dior Baby ski boots, well, even the most exercise phobic lady can find herself thinking wistfully back to the days when one could wear paint-stained vests and sagging shorts to the gym instead of worrying whether retro Kappa or futuristic Nike was the look that week. Now the only thing you can wear a paint-splattered vest to do is to paint your front room. Everyone knows what body fascists personal trainers and gym receptionists can be. Well, take that level of snootiness and imagine it regarding gym outfits and you've got a whole new level of aggression that could surely inspire *Mean Girls 2*, Lindsay Lohan's freedom from prison notwithstanding.

Still, it's always nice to see that even supermodels find exercise a bit of a bore and seem only to drag their skinny butts out there these days to show that they, too, have, like, totally got into this new layering of vests schtick.

Fashion shows, *Darwin in motion*

*S*ome people find that looking up at the great black sky peppered with stars gives them a vertiginous sense of their own smallness in the great scheme of things. These people have clearly never been to a fashion show which would have taught them that long before.

There is a general belief that fashion shows are somehow glamorous affairs. It's an idea perpetuated mainly by films (see *Films about fashion and why they are all (mainly) rubbish*) although seeing as movies about, say, London seem to think that the only habitable area is Notting Hill and that Dick van Dyke wasn't actually that far off on the ol' accent does suggest that perhaps we shouldn't take too many lessons from the silver screen.

In truth, fashion shows are brutally cruel affairs. They have nothing to do with the clothes: if they were about the fashion, designers could just put them on the internet instead of making the entire industry schlep about from New York, London, Milan and Paris twice a year and thereby saving everyone a lot of money and carbon footprints.

The real reason fashion shows exist is to teach everyone in the business their place. For designers, this comes from where on the schedule the fashion council puts their show: if it's at, say, 9 a.m., they are generally pretty much down there with Poundstretcher in terms of fashion credibility. Sometimes, though, this works in reverse, in that shows that are very important get the hated early morning slot, a clever ploy on the part of the schedulers to wrest the hungover journalists out of bed and away from their room service. How many people come to the show and who they are is also indicative of a designer's caste. Anna (Wintour, US *Vogue*), Cathy (Horyn, *The New York Times*), Suzy (Menkes, *International Herald Tribune*), Alexandra (Shulman, UK *Vogue*), Glenda (Bailey, US *Harper's Bazaar*), Carine (Roitfeld, French *Vogue*), Carla and Anna (Sozzani and Piaggi, Italian *Vogue*) and Katie (Grand, general fashion supremo) are pretty much the designer's dream front-row guests. A bunch of friends from fashion college and his mum are, rather heartlessly, not. The irony is that attendance is generally dictated by advertising (see *Advertising, how it spins the fashion axis*), in that if a designer advertises in a publication, that editor is forced to go to the show. Yet the only way a designer can afford to advertise is if they become successful, and the only way they can do that is to catch the eye of one of the above editor's eyes. To puzzle out that vicious circle could burst a blood vessel in the minds of gentler souls.

It's the journalists who get the harshest lessons, repeatedly, for four weeks, twice a year. There are few things that will teach you your place in the universe more swiftly than arriving at the entrance to the show, all decked out in the latest Alaïa, proving to your colleagues, that, yes, you know how to spend money, only for the eagerly awaiting paparazzi to look at you and, as one, lower their cameras in disappointment. This is usually followed by them all shouting at you to get out of the way because you are standing in front of that hot girl who was in *Aquaman 3 – The Fish is Back*.

Then you're in the tent. Yes, a tent. It is a rare fashion show that is in a posh salon: more often they're in a giant wedding marquee-style tent, or some horrible dark basement or, if the designer is just terribly 'edgy', in a cold warehouse in the middle of pig all nowhere, ideally in the dead of night and the depths of winter. You look at your ticket and here is when the proper humiliation starts. What

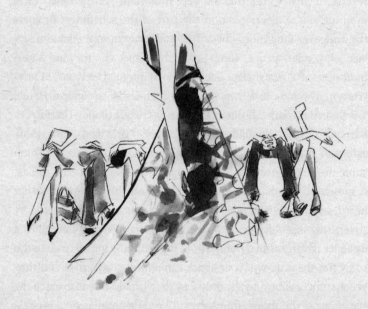

seat you've been given by the PR is a very public statement of your importance or otherwise in the industry. How this is decided is by processes both mysterious and incomprehensible. Fashion show seating arrangements are quite possibly one of the first matters of discussion at the Bilderburg Group conferences. Henry Kissinger in particular is said to be a real tyrant about them.

If you're in the front row, you must sit down immediately so that as many people as possible can see your positioning. Second and third row are bearable, as long as none of your colleagues are in front. Anywhere back from that and you have been well and truly cast out of paradise. Several options now await you. You can sit there and grouch to everyone around you about how at every other show you were in second row, the seating this time is crazy, I mean, look who's in third over there, I mean, they must have had the work experience girl do the seating this time, well, you won't be using any of the designer's clothes in your magazine this season, that's for sure.

Or you can cover up the number on your ticket and take a sly seat in the second row and hope that the person whose place it really is doesn't turn up.

Or you can force a grin, lump it and sit in your seat and pretend you are just above it all.

Or you can do what you really want to do and yell at the PR like a banshee, but you do have to weigh up the pros and cons on this option. On the plus side, it is rather satisfying and will probably get you a better seat next time around, if not now. On the downside, it can be rather humiliating to hear yourself having a temper tantrum in full public view about a chair.

Worst of all is if you see the dreaded 'ST' on your ticket. This means standing, as in, that's what you'll be doing at the back, as in, you're not even worthy of any chair, no, not even in the eighth row. You have absolutely no choice at this point but to leave the show and pretend you have been urgently called into the office.

So now you're in your seat at the precise moment the show is supposed to start, and you wait. And wait. And wait. And wait. When you get, say, a theatre or cinema ticket, the start time on the little slip of paper does tend to be exactly when your entertainment commences. The time on a fashion show ticket bears absolutely no relation to when the show will start, except maybe being within a general two-hour estimation and no one has yet come up with a satisfactory explanation of why this is. Yes, some people will make annoying noises about how it takes a while to get the models from show to show and then make them up in time and blah blah blah. But considering fashion shows have been taking place for about a hundred years you'd think that designers and schedulers would have realized this by now and come up with a realistic running time instead of telling audiences get to a '3 p.m.' show only to then make them wait, chewing on their knuckles with boredom, for the show's actual start at 4:39. The truth is, it is just another example of the kind of teenage-like attitude the dominates the industry (see *Drugs, the role thereof*) in that being late is somehow cool: the designer is basically saying, my time is more valuable than yours and I am just much busier than you, you lowly layabouts.

Sometimes, though, the show is running late because of a celebrity and this is pretty much the final nail in the journalist's ego's coffin.

Fashion journalists like to think that they are the most important people at the show and they sit on the sidelines like Roman emperors while the designer waits with bated breath to see if their manicured thumb will point up or down. They are disabused of this illusion when they are kept waiting for two hours (or have we already mentioned this?) because front-row guest Tori Spelling hasn't arrived yet. The fact is, a tiny paparazzi photo of a celebrity in the front row will do more for a designer's career than a front-page headline proclaiming his brilliance. The word 'irrelevant' haunts the journalist on many dark nights of the soul.

And then, at last, the show starts. And then it's over. Yes, all that fuss for a seven-minute event. In order to re-confirm one's sense of unimportance, the designer will then come out and give personal waves to the carefully chosen few. Then it's the mass exodus, with everyone who was so desperate to get in and be given their important seat now suddenly so consumed with desperation to leave you'd think polonium had been discovered on the premises. If you are important, you will have either a bouncer (for celebrities) or a dedicated minion (for fashion editors) to plough a path for you through the crowds to ease your exit. Everyone else will have to fight their own battle. But hurry! There's no time to waste! The next show starts in twenty minutes, you know!

Fashion *speak*

$\mathcal{T}$ he poet Joseph Parisi once said, 'Among the foremost repositories of demented language today are fashion magazines, art journals and the back covers of poetry books.' One can see where he's coming from, but Parisi rather overestimates the linguistic capabilities of art criticism and poetry publishing. Although both of those industries, particularly the former, rely heavily on the parlance of nonsense in order to maintain their elitist images, neither has managed to coin a lingua quite so unfrank(a) and so Saussurianally disconnected from the real world as fashion speak. After all, this is an industry that runs on a schedule predicated on some previously unknown timescale that consists of only two seasons a year called 'autumn/winter' and 'spring/summer'.

Latinate in origin, Chinese in incomprehensibility, fashion speak is a lot like an onion in that it contains many layers that merely conceal more layers, it can cause tears of frustration and it just keeps repeating on you no matter how grimly you swallowed it down last time.

But before you stroll down the easy path of mockery, take pause and consider the actually fairly justifiable reasons for its existence. For a start, trends are, as they say, circular in nature (fashion speak for 'frequently regurgitated') and there are only so many times a person can say 'Pencil skirts are back' before the will to live seeps from their saggy, despairing being. So thank God for coinages such as 'It's all about the fifties' (see *Decade rehashing, and why designers live in the past*) and 'The sexy secretary is huge this season', no matter how nonsensical or out of context they may well be.

Next, the majority of fashion journalists are not specifically trained in their field, unless a lifetime of shopping counts. And so, not entirely unlike the psychotic government officials from Orwell's apocalyptic vision of the future in 1984, they rely on an empty lingo to create a veneer of knowledge and professionalism and, most of all, for a bit of variety instead of just repeating what they really mean, which is 'I quite like these clothes, they would look good on me', which admittedly might have a kind of novel honesty to it but would get a bit tedious repeated twice a day, every day, for fifty years.

Finally, fashion shows run very, very late. On a typical fashion week day, the poor, huddled masses will spend approximately eight hours and forty-seven minutes gazing into dead space, tapping their pens against their carefully chosen Smythson notebooks, waiting for a wretched show to begin. Thus, a lady or gent has a lot of time to think deep thoughts, such as exciting new synonyms for words like 'beige' and 'good' in the same space of time in which they could probably find the cure for cancer.

'Homage' is probably the most well-known bit of fashion speak. A conveniently trussed up word for 'blatant copy', it can be used without the niggling fear of litigation and it has a soothing sheen of intellectualism, as though one is suggesting the designer in question spent long and noble hours in some dusty library, studying the technique of his forebears and then respectfully putting it into practice in his own noble work, as opposed to desperately ripping off someone due to a dearth of new ideas. For example, 'A-certain-designer-who-shall-remain-unlibellously-anonymous's homage to Courreges was perhaps a little over-literal.' Thus, it becomes a criticism in a compliment inside a totally daft remark, showing the kind of linguistic ingenuity that would make Derrida bow down in respectful awe.

Closely related is 'inspiration', used to denote the desperate recourse of a designer who has still not come up with any ideas two weeks before the collection is due. Off they hie hence to their teenage music obsession, a cinematic hero of old currently enjoying a bit of a renaissance or a painting in some heavily publicized exhibition at their local museum and then copy the bejeezus out of it. As in, 'Golly, Gucci really got a lot of inspiration from David Bowie this season.'

'Channel' is another useful term here. It sounds like a term a TV psychic might use when claiming an ability to resurrect the spirit of a dead person through their body and, actually, it does mean something like that. In the fashion world 'to channel' means that one is deliberately styling oneself to look like someone else, usually a dead former style icon, as in 'You might wonder why I am wearing a multicoloured chiffon kaftan and oversized sunglasses in London in November but I am totally channelling Talitha Getty this season.'

Fashion speak is essentially about giving an aura of gravity to what is undeniably a frivolous pursuit. 'Invest' is one such example, implying that getting another Whistles party dress is on a par with prudently buying stocks, as in, 'Yes, that £300 dress is a bit on the pricey side but, you know, it will be a great investment.' Similarly, 'archive' – or 'put into storage' to most people – is a more advanced example and, as such, is used mainly by the well-practised fashion linguists, i.e. the American fashion press and models. It gloriously conflates one's wardrobe with, say, a library of medieval manuscripts, as in, 'It's a shame that all of my wrap dresses have gone out of style this season so I'll just archive them.'

'This season's essential' or 'must have' is the baseline of fashion writing. And, really, one's response can only be, bossy, bossy, bossy! Fashion people love a good imperative, maybe because this kind of fearsomely brook-no-argument tone helps to trample over any bleating objections or queries as to why a £1,500 handbag with a handle made from the bone of a woolly mammoth and stitching from the hair of an albino virgin is apparently as necessary to someone's life as water. But there is some literal truth in the phrase as it is usually used in connection to this season's most expensive accessory by a company which has spent a particularly large wodge on advertising this season, the sort of advertising a magazine must, ahem, have.

Another good one is 'experimentation is key'. This is the telltale phrase that the designer or fashion journalist hasn't a freaking clue, or is hedging some unlikely bets, as in, 'Should you have a short waist but a long torso you should wear bias-cut skirts, but experimentation is key' and 'this season's de rigeur shade of bright mandarin looks just great against most complexions but experimentation is key'. I recommend using this handy phrase in all walks of life, not just fashion, e.g. 'Honey, do you know how on earth you fill out these tax forms?' 'Hey, experimentation is key!'

It is in descriptions of collections that the essentially euphemistic nature of fashion speak comes into its own. To describe a collection as 'very editorial' means that, as the designer appears to have taken the gimp from *Pulp Fiction* as his style inspiration this season, the clothes could only work in some edgy fashion shoot and won't ever see the light of production. Conversely, 'very commercial' means the clothes are very boring and all those beige trousers and black coats will sell by the bucket load in (sniff) middle America.

The various terms of approval of a collection are plentiful, reflecting the essentially positive nature of fashion journalism (see *Advertising, how it spins the fashion axis*). 'Spot-on', for example, is 'good', but with a gratifyingly bossy ring. 'Modern' means 'a bit different from last season'; ditto for 'vibrant', which is basically 'modern' but with extra colours, and maybe a frill, and ditto for 'fresh', which is exactly the same except perhaps with particularly young models in the show. 'Witty' is a polite word for 'so gimmicky even Timmy Mallett would balk at wearing it', 'Daring' is the synonymn for 'unwearable' as in 'A certain British designer's collection of balloon clothes was excitingly daring.'

'Romantic' and occasionally 'whimsical' can be read as 'simperingly floral'. All of these terms are used with notable frequency by the American fashion press in particular, who perhaps have starved themselves to such an extent that the oxygen is no longer reaching the brain area. The Brits might look like a bunch of fat trouts next to them, but at least they remember how to use the English language.

Colours allow designers and fashion writers to indulge their thwarted teenage poetic longings. 'Taupe', 'camel', 'putty', 'oatmeal', 'biscuit', 'sand' and 'nude' are all 'beige'; 'ivory', 'snow', 'virginal' and 'oyster' are 'white'; 'cherry blossom', 'blush', 'flush' are all 'pink'; jewels are always useful as in 'emerald' for 'green' or 'sapphire' for 'blue', although in the latter instance, should you be going for a more cerebral element it is better to say 'very Yves Klein'. Perhaps most poetically, 'cappuccino' is better known to the masses as 'pale brown'. Cruder mouths might refer to this kind of adjectivalizing as 'gold-plating some dung' but as long as the dung is described as 'mocha' no one will feel affronted.

There is even a word for the use of colour, full stop. 'Pop' basically means 'some colour in an otherwise dull outfit' as in 'Sharon Stone livened up her LBD with a pop of colour from her red belt.' 'Shot through' is another popular one, adding a bit of dynamism to what is otherwise an immobile piece of clothing, e.g. 'Dolce & Gabbana's black miniskirts were shot through with a hint of silver.'

Textures, too, come in for some gold-plating treatment. 'Butter soft' is a particularly popular one at the moment. It is only ever used in regard to leather, which, in reality, tends to be more smooth than soft and not generally reminiscent of a melting dairy product. 'Dove grey' is another unusual choice of reference point as doves are generally considered to be white. But maybe a lot of fashion people are colour-blind, which would, at least, explain the enduring appeal of Pucci.

And, finally, perhaps the most deceptive element of fashion speak is that the same terms and words take on different meanings depending on from whose mouth they emerge. The most complex one is when someone describes something as 'in'. When a fashion person (from here on referred to as FP) says this, they mean something that only they, a few select other FPs and the girl in the Balenciaga advert are wearing. When anyone else does, they mean something currently sported by them, half of the teenagers on Oxford Street and the mannequins in the windows of New Look. Proof if proof were needed that just because you can speak the language it does not mean you will as yet have access to the inner sanctum. You didn't think it was that easy, surely?

Festivals, *and why they're a bit like being pregnant*

*T*here was a time when a person at a music festival was considered quite the definition of high-maintenance chic if they put their dog on a lead instead of favouring the more traditional muddy string method.

Now that festivals have been taken over by musicians' model girlfriends and tickets are so expensive they can only be bought by west London trustafarians and the upper middle classes, they have become a veritable fashion industry in themselves, with Glastonbury being the *Vogue* of the circuit. Every year, the British fashion press greets the advent of summer with the traditional 'What to wear at a festival' feature, in which helpful suggestions like 'Go for the layered look' tend to be made, usually illustrated by a Marc by Marc Jacobs puffa jacket (£360 for you, good madam) and a Bella Freud jumper dress (£450, ta). And even if there wasn't the risk of bumping into Kate Moss down in the mosh pit wearing a Biba minidress and an oversized cardigan from one of McQueen's first collections, there are now additional fashion pressures. Newspaper photos of lithe young lovelies lounging in the sun or, even better, rolling about in the mud is a guaranteed winner in the slow summer months. Thus, canny festival goers with an eye on newspaper front-page fame know that it's worth opting for a mini floral skirt, bare legs and wellies instead of the usual jeans and hooded sweatshirt approach, even if it does mean they will probably catch hypothermia and God only knows what in the Portaloos.

In the main, though, clothes at festivals haven't changed that much – it's just that the extremes have become more marked. So those who look effortlessly fabulous on a daily basis in their normal lives look annoyingly fabulous sloshing about in the Glastonbury mud decked in several cropped jumpers they picked up from Portobello, layers of Victorian slips they found in Mummy's attic, and a fabulous pair of Wellingtons that make their legs look even thinner than usual. The rest of us, however, spend seventy-two hours in some badly fitted jeans, our older brother's discarded Gap hoodies and trainers that prove one needn't go to war to get a tasty dose of trench foot. In this way, festival dressing has become a bit like maternity wear in that we are now told that it's all gone very fashion and one now has to wear maternity Seven jeans and Juicy Couture tunic tops in order to be accepted by one's fellow sufferers. Such diktats may well be embraced by those to whom such diligence comes naturally. The remaining 99.99 per cent of the population, however, happily use the occasion as an excuse to dress how, secretly, we all occasionally wish we could all year round: like homeless slobs for whom the words 'waistband', 'high heel' and 'colour coordination' have as much relevance to one's life as 'juice fast'.

In point of fact, the festival as a whole has many similarities with being pregnant: you're physically uncomfortable, you're surrounded by people who are younger, thinner and more energetic than you and you feel like you spend your life looking for a loo. But, as with pregnancy, there is generally a happy ending. For a start, unless you've accidentally bought tickets for a threstival (a festival dominated by smug parents pushing around their three-wheeled buggy;

KT Tunstall will be on the bill, if you're unsure), they are good fun, but only – and I realize this is somewhat maverick advice from a fashion book – if you totally give up all thoughts of fashion. The only important things to ask yourself when robing yourself for a day at a festival are: will this keep me warm, will this keep me dry, will this keep me protected in the Portaloo (i.e. no flip flops)? Thus, you are highly advised to model yourself on one of the magic mushrooms you will be offered as soon as you arrive by decking yourself in a luminous waterproof poncho (will make it easier for your friends to find you) and wearing sludge-coloured trousers to help the mud blend in that little bit easier. Don't wear anything knitted as you will smell like a manky cat when it – as it always will – rains. You should take one tip from your more fashion-fabulous fellow attendees in that Wellingtons are strongly advised, if only because they'll make it easier to kick people out of the way in the queue for a jacket potato. This will mean giving up your dreams of appearing on the front page of the *Daily Telegraph*, but life is full of such sacrifices. And, yes, you will look a complete fool but, come three in the morning, while the more delicate flowers are shivering pathetically in their vintage slip dresses, you can snigger up your chunky parka sleeve and will be able to carry on regardless, accruing all sorts of anecdotes, the majority of which will probably involve Bobby Gillespie. And don't be cowed by the celebrities: they all get to stay in the VIP area which probably has running hot water, central heating, walk-in wardrobes and, for all I know, personal stylists on tap. After all, even Kate Moss could catch trench foot. Bobby Gillespie, however, is probably superhuman.

Films about fashion *and why they are all (mainly) rubbish*

*F*unny thing, this issue about fashion in movies. Seeing as the former is an industry based on visuals you'd think that there would be few other subjects that would lend themselves so easily to being depicted on screen. Yet from *Designing Women* to *Funny Face* to *Prêt-à-Porter* to *The Devil Wears Prada* there has yet to be a movie about the fashion business that is less shallow than the world it purports to cleverly depict and sardonically critique, simply because they universally rehash more creaky clichés than a whole week's worth of ITV sitcoms. Let's see, there's the harridan of a boss, bitchy journalists who never eat and seem to be able to afford Chanel couture despite earning about £3 a day, sleazy photographers, queeny designers and expensive freebies raining down like wedding confetti. Honestly, at least you could do your subject matter the honour of making up some jokes that haven't been getting wheeled out since the Churchill years. Even Rodney Dangerfield updated his set every couple of decades. Surely it couldn't be that the film-makers themselves get so distracted by all the glitz and pomp they're allegedly satirizing that their brain is rendered momentarily incapable of thinking of any new jokes or seeing past the surface?

God knows the fashion world has its absurdities and it is a lot easier to send up than, say, peacekeeping missions in the Middle East. So, yes, showing a big editorial meeting in which the topic up for solemn discussion is whether one should do a double-page spread of red shoes or blue hats might have a kind of novel appeal for a film-maker. But that is what these magazines are about, as anyone who opens one can see: it's not necessarily any more surreal than showing the editorial meeting of a car magazine, say, in which the hot topic for discussion is whether a man should go for bucket seats or leather upholstery. The word 'illuminating' is not generally one that comes to mind when watching a movie about the fashion business.

Aside from the staleness of the jokes it's the not exactly subtle underlying message that grates.

Movies about fashion always make fun of or punish the women who work – very successfully, incidentally – in an industry they enjoy. In *The Devil Wears Prada*, for example, the Anna Wintourish magazine editor might be the most powerful woman in fashion, but her husband leaves her, because, as far as can be ascertained, she had the temerity to be late for dinner occasionally due to work obligations. In an almost identical plot in *Sex and the City*, Carrie's magazine editor is often spotted having lonely solo lunches or hiding shyly in the corners at parties, and the only human relationship in her life is with a man whom she has to share with another, younger, woman.

And it's not just that they work in any industry, but in one that is dominated by other females. Oooh, scary! It's like some sci-fi dystopian nightmare! Thus, fashion magazine employees are invariably depicted as childish, narcissistic bitches. See what happens when you let the silly billies work together in a closed environment? Give them a second and they'll start lobbing sanitary towels at each other. Hence the inevitable character of the friendly, often gay, man in the office, usually working as the art director or something vaguely masculine. Sure, he might have chosen to work in fashion, but at least he's not riddled with oestrogen.

Career women rarely come off well in movies anyway: a snog with a generic leading man is still generally viewed as the happy ending to aim for; a promotion or deal clinch is merely compensating gloss on an otherwise lonely life spent eating TV dinners in front of *Friends*. But this is particularly true in movies about fashion because the fashion industry is generally seen as pretty silly, so film-makers can get away with more. Thus, a woman who seriously devotes her life to it, instead of concentrating on acting all Sandra

Bullockishly kooky and charming with every passing man, can more easily be depicted as being blind to the important things in life and a self-deluding bitch.

As has been said before in this book, fashion is a billion-dollar industry and it would be awfully hard to keep that afloat if the main movers and shakers inside it sat around all day fretting whether the high sugar content in grapes would make them fat, pausing only to try to stab one another in the back.

This is not a plea for fashion to be taken more seriously, nor even a whinge about the injustice to fashion assistants by Hollywood, which, as causes go, is probably not up there with calls for racial tolerance. But fashion on many levels magnifies female issues in popular culture, from the exaggerated body fascism in the industry to the interest in self-expression through physical appearance. So the wholesale dismissal in film of women who work in fashion shows up the very outdated misogyny one still sees in pop culture about successful women, and women doing something that has shockingly nothing to do with men.

The fact that these films and TV shows don't come within ten miles of anything approaching accuracy is a much more minor niggle. Still, skinny women in Roland Mouret dresses sniping at each other in white-walled offices makes for a better scene than, say, a stylist's assistant packing up boxes of clothes in the fashion cupboard or a woman – gasp! – finding personal fulfilment from working in an industry dominated by powerful and, by and large, admirable ladies. And that's the main thing, right?

Flat boots, *good or a little bit Nazi?*

*T*here are undoubted military associations to the flat boot, particularly fascist ones if yours are, as they should be, long and narrow. Ooh, those Nazis knew all about how to give good leg shape, they did. But as long as your boots are not too (a) shiny; (b) clunky; (c) prone to being kicked in other people's faces, it's unlikely that anyone will confuse you with Goebbels. As much as everyone delights in reeling back in horror when an attention-seeking designer claims to have found inspiration in, say, the homeless (ahGallianochoo!), in truth, flat-boot designers are not trying to raise the spectre of Goering. There's just not that much money in that look these days, what with the National Front not yet being *Vogue* cover stars and all.

Flat boots are marvellous because they have all the comforts of normal flats yet give your legs more definition. And they are far better to be worn over jeans than high-heeled boots which just make everyone look like they are prance-prance-prancing My Little Ponies. Some women fear that they will make them look like they are in a marching band but as long as they are not paired with any red items with brass buttons you should be fine. And don't march.

Yet it's not all good. When a designer knocks out the flat boot he is more often than not evoking what he calls 'the equestrian look'. Designers love the equestrian look, not because they idolize Frankie Dettori (although that man is just fabulous at keeping his weight down), but because they align it with the upper classes. Unlike a lot of people, when designers talk about the upper classes, they don't mean the unattractive, dull-witted, incestuous sorts you'd find in an Evelyn Waugh novel, but rather the breezy arrogant types Helena Bonham-Carter used to play in movies before she stopped brushing her hair. Mainly this is because they think these are the people who can afford their clothes, when, in fact, as pretty much everyone else knows, these old-school aristos tend to be utterly broke due to not having worked for the past thousand years and having spent all the inheritance on heroin and having the roof fixed.

Flat boots with superfluous buckles and buttons down the side are classic examples of the equestrian look.

Another kind of flat boot that has equally odd and one would have thought anachronistic associations is the chunky flat boot. The Ugg, the extra wide-mouthed Wellington and anything fur-lined falls into this category in that they are deliberately capacious in order to make the calf look as thin as possible, like a little toothpick sticking out of a sickly cocktail. Now, as tactics go, it isn't exactly subtle, but it is very effective. However, once you notice that it makes you look like you are about to be sent to sleep with the fishes it is hard to maintain your awe for that little stylistic trick.

Flat boots should, by rights, be one of the most basic things in your wardrobe. It's when people start trying to (insert waving jazz hands movement here) liven them up a bit with buckles and buttons and fur that they became utterly ridiculous (see *Classics with a twist*). Granted, Ugg boots are ever so cosy, but I'm afraid they are another example of some fashion item that has been totally ruined by bad celebrity association (see *Celebrities, and when bad ones happen to good fashion*). And as for men wearing Uggs, there should be a law. Literally, a law.

Fur, bad, *and definitely a little bit Nazi*

*L*et's make this a quick one, shall we? Unless you are an Eskimo, or maybe following the route of the Trans-Siberian Railway on foot in January as a gap-year project, there is no excuse for fur, not now, not ever. Look, you know the facts and if you don't here they are summed up in speed-readable form: electrocution, anal probes, drowning, strangulation, tiny coops, orphans, skinned foetuses, forced abortions, blinding, beating, death, death, death. If anyone tells you that their pelt is the 'by-product' of the meat industry five out of ten times they're wrong and four out of ten they're lying and the remaining one time is pretty much impossible to verify. And what is known in the trade as The Vintage Excuse – when a person tries to justify their ratty old stole by saying that it's vintage therefore the animal was, um, dead already, as opposed to non-vintage furs which are apparently still alive – is untenable simply because the sales of any fur, vintage or not, promotes the look and feeds the industry. This basically means that gullible clothing retailers and fashion fuzzbrains will see you wearing it, potentially think that it is now acceptable and the trend will re-emerge. This goes a million times more so for celebrities who might think that they're displaying a vaguely dangerous air by throwing normal considerations to the wind and going out to the Ivy in their new chinchilla coat, when actually all they're doing is proving a long held theory that anyone who wants to be a celebrity in the first place, who finds that their existence is only vindicated by being photographed, is quite likely to be emotionally, mentally and intellectually subnormal.

Granted, it is hard to condemn fur, but still wear leather. But leather is much trickier to live without and a truly decent alternative that does not have some gratingly pun-tastic name has yet to be invented. Fur, however, is pretty darn easy to do without. Some of us have got by for several decades without wearing any and have yet to suffer hypothermia or feelings of fashion ignominy.

Fur supporters like to claim that they 'have' to wear fur because it just keeps them so darn cosy. Americans, who are more pro-fur than the Brits, are particularly fond of this justification and, yes, absolutely, parts of that country can be very cold indeed come winter. But, last I heard, New York, for example, does have access to this new-fangled invention called 'central heating'. Fair enough, it does only exist inside but seeing as the sole New Yorkers who spend any more than 10 per cent of their day not inside an office, apartment, coffee shop or taxi are homeless people, and this is rarely the demographic arguing the case for their Fendi arctic fox stole, it's a toughie of an argument to maintain.

The other appeal of pelts is that they show off wealth. Second only to jewellery (see *Jewellery, and when fashion just gets obnoxious*), nothing shows off concentrated high and superfluous expenditure than a big ol' fur, which might explain the remarkable number of cross-overs between the jewellery and fur customer bases. Just a fur trim can add hundreds, even thousands of pounds to an outfit, and all for the sake of having slightly warmer wrists.

As for arguments that wearing fur is 'natural', as proven by the fact our forebears wore it when they went out hunting woolly mammoths, two replies come to mind. First, this harks back to a time when the term 'central heating' referred to two sticks rubbing up against each other in the middle of a cave and the glaciers were only just beginning to melt, whereas now we have managed to globally heat up this planet so effectively it's a wonder we need coats at all, let alone fur ones. And, second, scary baddies in children's stories almost invariably wear fur, epitomized, of course, by Cruella de Vil, proving that it is instinctive human nature to equate fur-wearing with evil. And if the fur coat is trimmed with little heads and paws, presumably to keep the wearer company when all sentient human beings have moved away from her in disgust, you can pretty much assume you're dealing with a full on loon.

Comparing a woman wearing a Blackglama mink coat to the Third Reich might be a good example of how to take an argument too far and thus niftily destroy it, but just stay with me for a moment. You are literally wearing the skin of an animal. You are wrapping yourself inside a casing that once contained all the blood, guts and muscle. To not only desire this, but to spend thousands of pounds to achieve this betrays a mentality so devoid of any thought beyond one's own preening, narcissistic comfort that vague memories of facts from GCSE history about the Nazis making lampshades out of Jews' skins cannot but creep to mind. A little extreme, yes, but you have to admit, there is something deeply weird about wanting to wear the skin of a former living thing.

Most people remember that Naomi Campbell and Cindy Crawford vowed that they would 'rather go naked than wear fur' when they posed for a campaign for PETA, only then to turn around a few years later and discover that, actually, the latter option wasn't looking too bad these days. Less well known is how these splendid gals justified this turnaround. Crawford, for one, dismissed the public criticism via her publicist, saying that she had never really supported PETA's stand against fur, but was instead being 'really nice' to the organization when she posed for its campaign in the nineties. Campbell, meanwhile, carried on regardless and is now more commonly seen in court up on charges for her after-hours hobby of slugging her personal assistants with her bejewelled BlackBerry.

Now I ask you, do you really want to show the world you share the same aesthetic tastes with two such dames? And that's really the main problem with fur, in my esteemed opinion: never mind the anal probes, it's the demographic you join by wearing it.

G-strings, *and the female lie*

*N*ow, there ain't nothing like a bit of VPL to make one's backside look three times its normal size and for this reason women give prostrated thanks for the G-string (though hopefully not while they're wearing one – that would be just disgusting). Anything silk, some light cottons and the occasional pair of trousers would otherwise be rendered all but unwearable were it not for that bit of anal dental floss. One can't help but think that if these particular clothes were properly made, i.e. had decent inside lining and so on, then this wouldn't even be an issue but that, we'll just have to accept, is by the by.

Anyway, somewhere along the line it was decreed that men find this sexy, that looking at a woman with a bit of cotton thread stuck up her bum was the apogee of eroticism. And once Mel Blatt, she of the former All Saints parish, was photographed bending over with her G-string hoiked above her jeans waistband, well, the nation's women, possibly under mass hypnosis, instantly perceived this as simply the chicest look in town. My gosh, the clever thinking behind it! To hoik one's G-string shows, first, you are wearing one and, second, that it is now shoved so far up inside you could probably giving yourself a colonoscopy while ordering another mojito in the Met Bar. Yes, it was the age of multitasking.

This also cements the lie that women just love to wear strings all the time, denim not generally being a risk for VPL, because secretly, you know, we all just want to dress like bargain basement porn stars. They became yet another example of women wearing something uncomfortable purely for the sake of looking what they think men might find sexy. Men, meanwhile, shruggingly accepted that it must somehow be in women's biological make-up to do this because they sure as hell wouldn't want to walk around all day with a bit of cotton stuck up their arse. Unless they are Peter Stringfellow, of course, a man with a name of nigh on Dickensian aptness.

It is not a sexy look and it is definitely not a daily one – it's an occasional necessity to be endured, like a padded bra or control top knickers. And as for G-string bikinis, well, all that needs to be said is, enjoy the sandy haemorrhoids.

Get, *fashion that girls do and boys don't*

*A*s anyone who's ever watched an episode of *Men Behaving Badly* or perhaps an old Sandra Bullock film knows, it is coma-inducingly dull to hash up old gender stereotypes of the, gosh, aren't men crap / women brilliant / men sensible / women mad variety. But it seems unlikely that membership of the gender equality movement will be revoked for stating that sometimes women wear clothes that men just don't get.

Probably the prime example of this is patterns. You see a patterned

dress and think, Golly, isn't that summer dress with an old Liberty print rather fabulously kitsch, with its connotations of England of yore? He thinks, How about that? I never noticed how much she resembles my grandmother's sofa. Ditto with wedges: you're thinking, kinda cool in a fifties pin-up kinda way; he's thinking, hmmm, orthopaedic shoes, just like Old Mother Hubbard probably wore. Prom skirts – how fun and they make my legs look thin, versus why is she dressed like the mother in *Back to the Future*?

And so the list goes on: tunic dresses, empire lines, cocoon and egg-shaped skirts and dresses, anything with superfluous buckles and bows, handbags the size of TV sets.

And a response along the lines of 'so the hell what' really does come to mind. First, the idea of only buying clothes that make you look thinner, taller, bustier or a little like Jennifer Aniston (pre-pity era) evokes an existence so joyless it makes knowing what a glycaemic load is sound like quite a reasonable use of one's brain cells.

If, however, your self-esteem is not predicated on the male gaze, then wear your patterned skirt, pussy-bowed blouse and your new wedges and enjoy working that (admittedly, a little too literal) retro secretary look you got going down. Fashion is about self-expression and if your self has a little more going for it than worrying about what pleases either of the two pillars of fashion dictatorship – men's mags (tight, short, available) or TV style makeover shows (fluted sleeves, bias cuts, unthreatening) – then show it to the world and if they don't like it that's just too damn bad. It's your money and your wardrobe space. Fashion should be something that gives you pleasure; it should not be a logic puzzle to master every morning: 'OK, as I've got short arms I need mid-length sleeves, and, with the shape of my legs, I have to find a knee-length skirt.' It's getting dressed, not flipping Tetris.

Moreover, sometimes it's fun just to get on with the fashion trend and to communicate through secret sartorial symbols to other members of our own gender that we, too, read that article in *Glamour* saying we should all try ankle boots with cashmere tights this month.

And shouldn't we applaud this? Is it not heartening to realize that sisters are, indeed, doing it for themselves? The rise of labels like the wonky-but-wonderful Marni and frumpy-but-fabulous Prada just proves how deeply this shift has occurred in fashion and women's approach to fashion in general. Here are two fashion labels that require one to put on one's fashion goggles (a.k.a. to have read a fashion magazine) in order to realize you're looking at fashion at all instead of, say, some plain jumpers or baggy tunic dresses. But women love them. And that is why it's call womenswear: it's for the women who wear it. Otherwise it would be called maleonlookers-wear and that's just clunky.

This is not to say that one should ignore male opinion entirely. A man can be extraordinarily useful as a voice of reason should you get a little carried away, sartorially speaking. With the noble exceptions of Zandra Rhodes and Italian *Vogue* fashion editor Anna Piaggi, few women really want to go out in an outfit that risks causing years of trauma to passing children. But, equally, this does not mean that one should completely quash one's own personal taste. Without wishing to drop an actually-Pamela-Anderson's-aren't-real-sized bombshell on any male readers, not everything women do is for men. Anyway, it's not as if women sit around wondering why men make themselves deliberately fat and smelly by sitting around all weekend in darkened rooms watching *Match of the Day* like inert bullfrogs. And so, male readers, now another phrase is coming to mind. Wait a minute . . . here it comes . . . oh yes: 'Deal.'

Hair accessories, *gimmicks for reluctant adults*

*D*efinitely one of the more clever offshoots of the accessories madness (see *Accessories, going to hell in a handbag*). Designers wisely prepared the ground for this state of affairs with the ever rising costs of accessories in general, but designer hair accessories are truly the heroin of the fashion industry in that they must be the ultimate example of 1000 per cent mark-ups. A lovely young British woman called Katie Hillier can take a lot of credit for this as she is the woman behind many of the pieces that the king and queen of tempting knick-knacks, Marc Jacobs and Luella, have been knocking out for years, particularly their oversized logoed hair baubles. Miu Miu and Prada, similarly, have been making pretty feathered and glitter Alice bands for some time, convincing women who really should know better to pay triple figures for – and I would like to emphasize this for a second time – an Alice band. Aside from the fact that you are likely to lose your designer hair accessory after one wear, they are not quite as daft as you think: a pretty hair accessory distracts from a bad haircut / day / life and a sparkly hair band will do more than a gallon of Touche Eclat. Feathered Alice bands, particularly ones that match the colour of your hair, are possibly the easiest way to add some pleasing glamour to an outfit that even you are sick of seeing yourself wearing. Frankly, it's a lot easier to stick an Alice band in your hair than figuring out how the hell one is supposed to put on liquid eyeliner without ending up resembling Marilyn Manson's female counterpart.

But it's the words 'Alice band' that cause a lot of women in this country to quail, and understandably so. One must always be on one's guard against the return of the Sloane and Alice bands, sadly, are very much the sartorial symbol of this demographic. A pity, really, because most women look better with their hair neatly tucked back. That so many of them often wear their sunglasses pushed up on their head proves that they themselves know this fact and they cowardly make do with this pathetic compromise just because they fear the stigma of the Alice band. Shake off the shackles of fear, you sad, repressed ladies, and just get yourself a pretty Alice band, either a jewelled, sequinned or feathered one or a simple black one. Never a plastic or wooden one, mind, as it will squeeze your head like some medieval torture instrument.

The difficulty with hair accessories in general is that they can easily shade into the paedo chic territory but this, too, is unfair. Quite why only children are allowed to sport things to keep their hair tidy when it is unquestionably adults who reap the harsher criticism for going around with hair best described as Winehouse-ian makes little sense. Not everyone has the time, money or patience for a weekly £100 blow dry, you know. Admittedly, the hair accessories industry has not helped itself on this score by decking the majority of hair baubles and whatnots with multicoloured charms and Hello Kitty characters but one must fight this vicious circle, if only for the noble cause of tidy hair. So step away from the pink hearts: you will only compound sceptics' prejudices against hairbands and simultaneously make yourself look like a complete twit. The only allowed kind are monochrome or black and white spheres, cubes or something similar and minimalist (well, as minimalist as you can get with a hair bauble).

Scrunchies manage to beat even the Alice band in terms of unfortunate image association. Forever associated with naff eighties aerobics classes and carpool mothers, it has defied the skills of even the most determined fashion stylist to resurrect this accessory, even on an ironic level. Unlike the beleaguered Alice band a scrunchie improves no one's look – it's sloppy, it's clunky and it doesn't even hold your hair in properly. *Quel*, as the French probably don't say, *est le point?*

Haircuts, *the meaning beneath the layers*

Thanks to that universal hairdresser opening spiel, we've all heard that haircuts are dependent on face shape. But, in truth, we all know that the only thing to bear in mind when choosing a haircut is what it says about you.

This is why women get so stressed about their hair. Aside from the general complaints pretty much every woman save Jemima Khan (the goddess of long hair) has regarding their hair, it is this tonsorial message that causes the angst. No single garment, nay, not even a word out of your mouth will create as much of an immediate first impression as your haircut. But, you know, no pressure.

The youthful pixie cut is one such example. Here is a haircut that says, 'I am young and I have heard the word "gamine" and I like it. I am ethereal and above material concerns like buying conditioner. But such spiritualism in no way conflicts with my desire to show off what I have been told are my very good cheekbones.' For the older woman, this cut tends to be indicative of an exchange of vanity for deeper, more cerebral concerns, as though you are too busy campaigning for Sudanese refugees or memorizing Shakespearean soliloquies to brush your hair in the mornings (ref: Judi Dench). But it can look a bit like you just can't be arsed any more.

The bob is an interesting one as this sends different messages depending on what side of the social spectrum you're coming from.

Because long hair is still synonymous with youth it's either the compromising style of a woman who reckons that her long feminine locks on which she relied for the first twenty-nine years of her life just aren't suitable any more, but she's not in any way ready for the middle-aged crop. Grown-up but still pretty, in other words, while wisely ducking the yummy mummy cliché of long hair swinging about one's shoulders in front of the school gates. Or it's the aspiration to thinking-girl status for a pop star or socialite, though it says something about both of these demographics that lopping off three inches of hair is considered proof of one's intelligence. Because the bob is a fairly limiting hairstyle it requires the same amount of confidence as the pixie cut because you are going to be stuck looking at the same reflection in the mirror for the next six months. For this reason, it is also very popular with women who are or just wish to look very professional and busy because there is absolutely nothing that needs to or can be done with it. Anna Wintour is the icon, Betty Boo is the occasional outcome.

The gateway to the bob, the fringe, works in a similar manner but with whole new levels of semiotics and suggestion. Somehow, this goody-two-shoes style has recently acquired an edgy kind of image. Once it brought to mind images of Baby Spice; now it is more redolent of the slightly cooler Karen from the 'Yeah Yeah Yeahs'. This is mainly because it works in the same way as the pixie cut and bob in that it is suggestive of confidence in one's appearance since, ultimately, once you have a fringe, there is not much more you can do to your hair as it's just going to sit there, like a pudding. Of course, the real boon of the fringe, which probably explains more fully its sudden popularity, is that it is painless Botox in its wrinkle coverage factor. In this sense, it is basically the posh version of what was once known, to use the probably not politically correct term, as the Croydon facelift, which involved pulling back one's hair into a ponytail so tight your face looked like Hans Solo's at the beginning of *Return of the Jedi* as he strained to get out of his wall tomb.

Because fringes themselves have become so popular even the type of fringe you have has become fraught with meaning: do you go for the 'I'm a bit quirky and did I mention I live in Shoreditch' slightly too short wonky style? Or perhaps the mainstream pop star diagonal long cut, perfect for looking up to the right and batting your MAC-coated eyelashes? Or maybe the Sloaney long and thick version, again, very useful for eyelash battage? Know thyself, choose thy fringe, as Yoda might well have said, should he have pondered the matter. The best kind is the long and thick version, but this does depend on you having quite thick hair to begin with, otherwise you will use up half the hair that should be around your skull to sit atop your forehead, which not only isn't very attractive, but just looks silly and creates what could almost be described as the female equivalent of the male combover. Aside from the thin-haired, the fringe also discriminates against curly ladies, I'm afraid: a curly fringe is a combination so wrong as to be almost oxymoronic, like celebrity perfume and Simply Red's *Greatest Hits*.

Layering is the bootcut jean of the tonsorial world with its mainstream feminine appeal, the obvious benefits (it vaguely makes your hair look thicker), but the equally pressing disadvantages (you now have completely uneven hair that will look a total state as soon as you try to grow it out). Yet, like the bootcut, such detractions have wielded notably little sway and layers continue to be the most popular style for women, possibly due to too many seminal years of watching Farrah Fawcett and her eighties aspirants flick their short and long bits around with such fabulous insouciance.

And then there's the most popular hairstyle of all for the British woman: the shoulder-length opt-out. This is the female hair equivalent of the commitment-phobic boy: you know you're getting on a bit, you know you really should let go of some of those hang-ups you've had since you were fifteen, but somehow you can't quite make the leap to having a proper haircut – too scary, too high maintenance, too expensive, you imagine. In fact, just as lurching aimlessly from relationship to relationship is probably more expensive and exhausting than just settling down, so having to get your shapeless shoulder-length style trimmed every six weeks is far more tedious and less heart-warming than embracing a proper cut.

But at least women can have a bit of fun with their hair without risking accusations of effeminacy or general pretension. Men undoubtedly have it much worse, mainly because they must work within a smaller framework and thus the slightest alteration from within has a much greater and potentially more damaging impact. There's the ageing Lothario quiff, which is when an older gent who walks through life with the optimistic words 'silver fox' dancing through his head and is so proud of maintaining his thick locks he quiffs them up to a gravity defying and denying degree (ref: Robert Redford, Warren Beatty).

This tendency to be so proud of one's assets that one then flaunts them to an inadvisable degree is a common mistake made by both men and women, in hair and non-hair matters. With women, it tends to be in regards to thinness or breast size, leading, in the case of the former, either to overly cinched dresses, too high miniskirts or scarily childlike clothes ('I'm so little I can still fit into Gap Kids, giggle giggle!'). The correct response to this is, 'Yeah, you must be really grateful that the childhood obesity problem has helped to widen your wardrobe choices.' In regards to mammary matters, the obvious result is a cleavage that rivals the Grand Canyon (see *Cleavage, and the plumbing of depths*).

Going back to men's hair, there's the 'head 'em off at the first post style', otherwise known as shaving your head at the initial sign of balding, as if, actually, you always intended to have a naked scalp so this is really a good thing and what do you mean you found a bottle of Just For Men in my bathroom? The short back and sides is always safe, if a little retro (fashion speak for 'dull') and the lightly feathered cut, a.k.a the male Judi Dench, tends to be favoured by self-conscious magazine editors, who think such geekiness is a bit, y'know, ironic.

No more need ever be said in regards to the combover ever since the truly seminal *Oprah Winfrey* show in which she cut off men's combovers. Oprah, not even that school you set up in Africa has ever demonstrated more succinctly why you were put on this planet.

Name me a single time when long hair has improved a man's looks and I will personally come round to your house and tap-dance naked on your coffee table. The absolute nadir is the long but balding cut, creating what can only be described as a kind of wilting crop circle effect on the gentleman's head. It is so easy to see the train of thought here: 'I know, I'll compensate for the lack of hair upon my head by growing it to hang around my jowls.' But as is always the case with fashion, when the intention is obvious, the effect is simply unacceptable (see *Animal print, when women roar*. Or for that matter, just see Status Quo's Francis Rossi.)

Haute couture, *taking self-indulgence to a whole new level*

*E*verything about the haute couture industry is self-indulgent: from the women spending £50,000 and seventy hours being measured for a single dress decked with gold tassles and beading; to the designers staging huge shows in which models visibly wilt under the weight of their Elizabethan ballgowns, crusader helmets and medieval weaponry-influenced accessories, all in the name of conveying the designer's self-professed fascination with 'strong women' (although, one is tempted to suggest, if they're so interested in strong women, how about instead of lumbering seven-stone models with oversized clothes in order to make them look bigger, why not just get some models who actually weigh more than one hundred pounds and therefore possibly have shoulders that consist of more than jutting twiggish bones?); to the journalists making the biannual schlep to the shows in Paris to write about clothes that, unless they work for *Majesty* magazine, not a single one of their readers will ever wear; to the celebrities shipped in to make their requisite front-row appearance all in the name of getting a bit more attention for themselves and the designer without even the mitigating possibility that they are likely to wear these clothes to anywhere other than the Oscars.

Most people's idea of fashion shows is based on the couture ones, not the relatively more proletariat prêt-à-porter. Couture is the perfume oil to prêt-à-porter's eau de parfum: a more concentrated version and, as such, with a decidedly stronger, occasionally over-powering, effect. Certainly prêt-à-porter has its moments, but fash-ion's long-maintained reputation for theatrical silliness would be seriously dented if people knew that the majority of the ready-to-wear shows involved models wearing plain trousers, floaty dresses and, in short, looking like normal women – conspicuously well-dressed women, admittedly – on their way to meet friends for lunch. So thank heavens for the pyrotechnics of couture to keep the fires of the old stereotypes burning brightly.

Just as every British fashion journalist has to write, at least twice a year, a half-hearted article weakly waving the flag for London Fashion Week, even though British fashion designers seem to have realized this is a lost cause judging from the way they all flee the city at the first sniff of success, so every fashion journalist in the world needs to write a biannual article justifying the ongoing couture industry. It's the price you pay for having found a way to make a career out of talking about dresses and shopping.

There's no real justification for couture – of course there isn't. Maybe back in Marie Antoinette's day when there was nothing to do but lie around all afternoon eating pastries, taxing peasants, and being fitted for one bed jacket, then perhaps spending more on a dress than most people earned in a lifetime made just the most mar-vellous sense. Now that we live in a Topshop Zara world, such a concept holds somewhat less allure.

The fact that the few people left on this planet who do have the time, money and capacity for such sheer self-indulgence are such an undeniably unappealing bunch has not helped couture's image. Minor European royals, overfed bankers' wives – the word 'aspirational' does not come to mind here.

The most commonly used justification for couture wheeled out by the desperate fashion hack is that it provides a 'springboard' for the designer's creativity as he can practise the more extreme variations of styles for next season in the welcoming hothouse of the couture world. Aside from the appealing image this argument conjures up of designers as mad scientists mixing crazy potions, this theory just does not wash. Of course designers need to experiment and, yes, they might need to work through various versions of a style before they arrive at the watered-down, wearable, conclusion. But why does a whole industry need to be based around what are essentially designers' first drafts?

The other argument is that couture is not fashion – it's art. The ol' 'Is fashion art' article is even more boring and tired than the 'What is the point of couture' one. Fashion has to be wearable, otherwise it is not clothes, it may as well be a medieval artefact in the Natural History Museum. Certainly the work that goes into couture clothes is impressive, judging from statements that buzz around the couture shows like pesky flies, such as, 'That dress took ninety hours for one seamstress to make,' and 'The beads on that bodice were culled from an endangered talking oyster.' But if it's just art, why is it tied to the commercial structure of fashion seasons? I doubt if Leonardo da Vinci ever thought, 'You know, I'd really fancy knocking out another painting this month, but it's October and I only produce my wares for the public twice a year in order to fit in with store ordering systems and fashion shoot schedules.'

The only justification for couture is that it's fun. Couture is the fashion world writ large, with its silly shows, its pretentious inspirations and its hilarious price tags. Thus, it demonstrates more clearly than anywhere else that the only point of fashion itself is to have fun. You can try to find as many justifications as you like, but, ultimately, it's about enjoying clothes, and there really is no other excuse at all for couture than that. You can't even use the vague excuse that you have for prêt-à-porter, which is that people need clothes therefore it is providing them a service: not even your average helmet-haired, wind-tunnelled-faced couture customer would claim that anyone actually needs a £30,000 bolero jacket. In short, couture is a sharp lesson in the realities of the fashion world and proof of how one just has to lean back and enjoy it. And if that means never having to read another article about whether fashion is art, or what the political significance of a long hem is, well, I'd say that it provides a darn good service to all mankind.

Heels, *the highs, the lows and when fat is better than thin*

*L*eaving aside for the moment the issue of heel height, heel width has become quite a big deal recently, literally and, um, topically. In short – and enjoy this sentence while you can, because you're unlikely to hear it in regards to anything else in the fashion world – fat is suddenly better than thin.

This, at first, would seem not to make a jot of sense. The whole theory behind heels – indeed, the only real excuse for them – is that men allegedly find them sexy. Now is not the time to delve too deeply into why any man would find a limping woman with an overly developed Barbie-doll-like foot arch attractive (or perhaps we might have just answered the question), but rather let us just accept that, if this is the case, then a thin, delicate heel is definitely sexier than a clunking great tubster.

A spindly spike continues the high-heel illusion that the woman is an airy Tinkerbell-like creature who can float through the air, carried only by toothpicks beneath her feet, such is her lightness – a delicate flower who never sweats, belches or bleeds.

With such unquestionable logic behind it the thin heel has been ubiquitous for some time now and, in the fashion world, down the path of ubiquity lies the grove of purdah. Hence the emergence of the thick heel.

The brilliant thing about the thick heel – aside from the fact that, after 2,000 years, shoemakers seem to have come to grips with the idea of weight distribution – is that it doesn't look like you're trying so hard to be sexy and this, in itself, is sexier.

This is why labels like Chloé (maternity dresses, odd high-waisted trousers, orthopaedic shoes) and Prada (librarians ahoy) are now considered to be as sexy as, say, Versace and Dolce & Gabbana were in the admittedly tackier if perhaps less hypocritical eighties.

Fashion magazines are very fond of using the word 'insouciance' in regards to this look, possibly because it sounds a bit French and it's quite fun to show off that you know how to spell it. 'Effortless' is another popular one, even if the word does chime a bit oddly when talking about a £600 Miu Miu boot and a £900 Marni sack dress.

Nevertheless, it does make a kind of sense: there is something undeniably tragic about seeing a woman teeter about on her spindly heels, like one of those funfair clowns that children try to knock over with plastic balls to win a stuffed donkey, all in the name of getting male approval (the woman on heels, that is, not the donkey-seeking children). A woman who wears thick heels, however, gives off an air of confidence, of knowing that she doesn't need toothpicks to get some.

The only exception to this thin is bad, fat is good rule is when it comes to what is known as, to use its Latin name, the Spark-lius Girlsnightoutus, otherwise known as the strappy sandal, which leaves the foot near naked with only a couple of strands of rhinestone or, for the classier sorts, leather ribbon ties to hold it in place. The strappy sandal is such a determined return to the obvious that to bother with all this faux frumpier-is-actually-sexier-than-sex nonsense would just be odd and pointless. It would be like eating a salad mid-chocolate pig out.

Another and perhaps less psychologically complex reason for the emergence of fat heels – and cone heels, while we're here, which are one step further down on the unsexy heel spectrum and, thus, a great favourite of 'insouciently' sexy womenswear designers like Marc Jacobs and Marni – is that they serve the same purpose as wedges and platforms in drawing attention to the shoe.

Women have long been a little weird about shoes and the cod Freudian theories behind this are too boring and too obvious to elaborate. (Oh, OK, fine: obviously, it's all about sex with all that insertion of the foot and penetration of the shoe, or whatever. God forbid women should do anything that is not somehow connected to sexual desire for a man as opposed to, say, just being materialistic and fancying a pair of shoes.) But this interest in showing off the shoe itself as opposed to how it makes the wearer look has emerged with the rise in accessory mania (see *Accessories, going to hell in a handbag*) in the past decade, when accessories became the main focus of the outfit as opposed to an afterthought. Well, if you're going to spend £400 on a pair of Burberry ankle boots, you might as well have people notice them.

The issue of heel height is a fraught one indeed. The famous, nigh on historical, really, 'fuck me shoes' stand-off between Germaine Greer and Suzanne Moore clarified two issues: one, perhaps the feminist movement wasn't working out too well if one of its leading lights was going around town like some ascetic Protestant priest casting the local girls on to the pyre for perceived whorishness. And, two, that after all these years, the feminist debate about fashion – conforming to a misogynistic interpretation of beauty versus women enjoying themselves – still hadn't been resolved. In fact, Germaine rather missed the point here because the issue about stilettos is not that the woman is betraying her feminist roots by trying to look like a slut; rather, it's that they suggest that she is totally daft and has absolutely no understanding of the concept of weight distribution and this, I'd have thought, is actually a worse betrayal of the equality dream.

It is the oddest concept, and it would have been interesting to see how it was first pitched: 'Hey, I know, guys! Let's make shoes that force women to walk on their tippy toes all day! Shoes that they cannot actually walk in; shoes that require them to take a taxi to travel to the end of the road!' 'Amazing! Crank up the machines!'

And yet, here we are, hundreds of millions of women hoisting themselves daily up on to the balls of their feet in the name of fashion, spending hundreds and hundreds and in some cases thousands

of pounds on shoes that they literally cannot walk in. 'Wow, loving your shoes!' 'Yeah, they're great. Can't really walk in them, of course, but they look fabulous.' Really, it's like saying, 'Yes, I love my new car. Of course, the engine is totally buggered, but I love to just sit in it not going anywhere.'

Stilettos make women:

(a) grumpy,
(b) lazy (due entirely to immobility),
(c) pathetically slow.

All, one would have thought, quite unattractive qualities. And yet, and yet, the myth persists that stilettos are sexy.

One theory is that they force the woman's foot into the shape it makes when having a Meg Ryan moment and thus gives off the image that she is sexually available. However, seeing as a woman mid-orgasm tends to be, shall we say, already taken and therefore the very opposite of available, one can only assume that what they really mean is that it suggests the woman puts out. Which is nice.

Others argue that the appeal of the high heel lies in the way it forces the woman's body into emphasizing her curvy, fertile shape. Kinda sweet, isn't it, to think that after all these years of evolution, all a man really wants to see is that his woman is fertile even if he doesn't actually – oh God, no, don't even raise the spectre of the possibility – want to have a child with her. Like I said, sweet. But perhaps women should ask themselves if they really want to walk around town looking like Nubian fertility symbols.

This is not to deny that high heels can be fun. Yes, they're glamorous and, yes, they're quite fun to dance in (for a few minutes, after which they become excruciating) as you can look down at your feet and pretend that you're Ginger Rogers. But accept that there is a downside to this heels nonsense and that the above listed negative elements sometimes cancel out the alleged positive ones.

The idea that stilettos are somehow 'dressier' and that flats are too 'casual' for a party is nonsense. There are so many pretty, dainty flats out there and so very many hideous, clunky, square-toed heels. Moreover, if you wear flats to a party you'll dash about all night like a veritable social dynamo, leaving men in your wake wondering who that fabulous creature was. Wear stilettos and you'll spend the evening slumped uncomfortably in the corner before you finally give it up, take off your shoes and show the world your cracked heels and hammer toes.

As for the kitten heel, really, the only thing to say here is that one should never trust anything with such a repulsively stupid name. What on earth could a squashed little heel have to do with the feline family?

Or could it, could it, possibly be that someone somewhere thought, 'Hmmm, how can I best flog this twee, winsome little heel to the clichéd vision of femininity for whom I've designed it? Maybe if I call it the naughty chocolate heel? The Chardonnay heel? The men are crap heel? No, wait, something's coming through – yes! The kitten heel!' Let's just be grateful they didn't call it the All Bar One heel.

The problem with the kitten heel is that, as happens with most compromises, you get the worst of both sides: you can hardly walk and you look about as sexy as a prancing duck. And this, as all ladies know, is not always a great look.

If you really are dead set on wearing a heel, get either a small-ish (but not kitten) slender one or a high one of a good four or five inches that is satisfyingly chunky because the higher the heel, the thicker the width, for both aesthetic and practical purposes.

But truly to see the cold reality of wearing heels just wait until the end of the party and watch the women leave. While those in flats glide easily out the door and dash lightly down the road to grab the last bus home, those in heels can barely hobble, their bodies limping slowly down the road, knees jutting forward, back hunching downwards, like homo sapiens emerging from the swamps. Thus, flat-wearers are, on all levels, more highly evolved. So there.

Jacobs, Marc, *genius or what?*

*G*enius, actually, since you ask, and not just because he makes such nice things that – shock, gasp – actually last for ever. Rather, it's how he has made a breathtakingly lucrative career for himself by mining an image for his label that is so utterly at odds with what he produces.

There are many other indicators of his brilliance – such as the way he made fashion cool again and is pretty much to thank for the rise of Topshop and the high street in general, both of which we'll get to in a bit – but number one has to be how he convinced the world that his label conveyed an image of downtown, cool creative chic, of young film directors having black coffee down on the Lower East Side as opposed to ritzied-up wives of bankers meeting for lunch at Barney's on Madison Avenue. Quite how £1,200 bags with giant gold chains and £3,000 floor-length dresses fit in with this idea of ascetic garret living is anyone's guess, but nonetheless Jacobs managed to convince the world that they were not incompatible. And how did he manage to do this? By palling around with Sofia Coppola (a Hollywood progeny who is seen as trendy primarily because she doesn't wear make-up and rarely smiles) and having Jurgen Teller (a hugely successful photographer who has a vaguely gritty reputation thanks to his wonky and frequently overly bleached pictures) shoot his advertising campaign. Wow, keep it real, Marc. At least the brand images of, for example, Dolce & Gabbana and Valentino (respectively, scary rich Italian ladies and scary rich European in general ladies) bear a modicum of truth in relation to their customer base. Marc Jacobs's brand image's demographic couldn't even afford to buy one of his key chains and the truth is a lot of the same people who buy Valentino also buy Marc Jacobs, it's just that they feel slightly cooler when they buy the latter.

In part, Jacobs's style and success reflects the general gentrification of New York City. Over the past fifteen years downtown has become just as chi chi as uptown, in the same way that the East End of London stopped being synonymous with mobster mass murders and more about overpriced artists' lofts. And just as the artists kid themselves that they're keeping it real by living amongst the People, even if the artists' presence has in fact priced out these valued People to the suburbs (and thank God – the People were a bit grubby anyway), so Jacobs's image is based on an idea of left-field artsy cool, not, as would probably be more accurate of both his downtown neighbourhood and customer demographic, trustfund kids ploughing Daddy's lifesavings into the ground.

Yet to mock is self-defeating because it is thanks to this truly impressive PR campaign that Jacobs regenerated the fashion world. Sure, fashion was always desirable, but by the early nineties it was all shoulder pads and ladies who lunch – profitable, perhaps, but not exactly cutting edge. Then scrawny, geeky, bespectacled Jacobs came along, put grunge on the catwalk, looked so much the opposite of, say, Gianni Versace that he may as well have been the photo negative of most people's image of a fashion designer, got photographed hanging out with cool celebrities like Sonic Youth and Evan Dando, made clothes for twenty-somethings as well as the older market and suddenly fashion became a young person's game. Labels such as Miu Miu, Luella, Stella McCartney and the rejuvenated Chloé all owe something to Jacobs because he really did pave a path, generally to the bank accounts of under twenty-five-year-olds around the world with trust funds.

And by making fashion younger, especially through his fantastic diffusion label Marc by Marc Jacobs, he also showed the high street how to make good clothes for teenagers that were a step above the scratchy cropped tops and saggy denim skirts it had been relying on previously. Topshop in particular has learned a lot from Jacobs (particularly his Marc by Marc Jacobs line), which is mainly not to underestimate the customer and that they do notice little details, such as oversized buttons and sleeves that are cut properly instead of bagging sloppily under the armpits.

With so many followers in his wake, perhaps it is understandable that Jacobs is concentrating these days on two ends of the spectrum: on the one hand, the more lah di dah end of the market with his mainline collections, and, on the other, the cheap and cheerful end with his diffusion label, knocking out heart-shaped plastic compacts and rubber beach shoes like he had never heard of the words 'image control', and thus increasingly leaving any pretensions to downtown hipster status out in the cold. He is now creative director of Louis Vuitton, perhaps the most shamelessly snooty label around, and has said that his dream job is to work at Chanel, the ultimate bastion of the very same ladies-who-lunch who controlled fashion before his grunged-up emergence. Plus ça change, eh? And yet, because he still looks like the school geek and still name-drops Sofia (who has moved on herself from slacker-tastic *Lost in Translation* to, rather aptly, *Marie Antoinette*), he is still seen as the acceptably cool face of fashion. Image, you know, is everything.

Jeans, *not as bulletproof as they tell you*

*A*h, bless the human species. No sooner does it find something pretty straightforward than it has to have a good fiddle about with it, divesting it of many of its original charms. Almost any dance remix of a good pop song comes to mind, as does the menu from a restaurant that goes by the handily catch-all name of 'fusion' or, most of all, anything described as a 'classic with a twist' (see aforementioned entry).

And so it has been with jeans. We all know the story: once jeans were kind of cool in a James Dean way; then they were the favoured uniform of the oddly deluded American tourist who seemed to think that wearing high-waisted tapered trousers in bleached denim was a sure way to cut a fine figure. And then in the nineties a clever little jeans label called Earl moved the waistband slightly lower, put a bit of stretch into the denim and – wham bam your receipt's in the bag, ma'am – jeans are suddenly the most flattering thing ever conceived in the history of civilization. New denim labels are launched seemingly every day with ever increasingly self-important names (Citizens of Humanity, True Religion, 7 for All Mankind – I mean, I ask you) and reported in the fashion press with the kind of hushed excitement that might lead you to believe that you are witnessing the unveiling of God's true form. Designer jeans now cost easily over £150, making them more expensive than a lot of designer shoes, yet this has not affected their popularity in the slightest.

And so manufacturers, understandably, decided to milk this cash cow for all it was worth, experimenting with every possible style, design and colour variation they could possibly imagine in order to keep convincing customers to buy more, more, MORE! Thus, what was once an easy basic became a fraught style statement with its own internal fashion trends.

The style that originally reeled in the masses was bootcut hipsters. The hipster element was clever because it differentiated them from the high-waisted yokel versions of old, thereby justifying their three-figure price tag. The bootcut was a little trickier. The theory behind this style is that by widening out the ankle the thigh will look proportionally slimmer. There is some merit in this but, really, you have to wonder about the intelligence of any onlooker who thinks, 'Wow, look how that lady's ankles seem to be about the same width as her thighs – golly, her thighs must be as thin as reeds! Hubba hubba!' The fact is, your thighs are still visible so it is only an optical illusion with a brief lifespan. If you really want to disguise your thighs, then you're going to have to wear wide-legged jeans and deal with the fact that you now resemble an extra in *On the Town*, the classic Gene Kelly musical about a bunch of sailors in New York.

Nonetheless, bootcut is still the most flattering denim style for most people. But, make no mistake, you are wearing denim flares, a style some of us thought we'd never see again outside of documentary footage of *Woodstock*.

Yet this is not what began to turn the fashion tide against the once seemingly all-mighty bootcut style, but rather simple overexposure. Because of its convenience and promises of instant slimness, it became as associated with yummy mummies as Chelsea tractors and daytime yoga classes. And so, as always happens with a fashion trend, an alternative was needed and it was an alternative few would have considered would ever succeed: *et voila*, the era of the skinny jean.

The skinny jean is manna from the fashion gods (or Selfridges, anyway) if you like to wear your boots over your jeans and for being able to check on the state of your cellulite without removing any of your clothes. What it's not so great for is anyone over a size 10. Just as 'bootcut' is just a fancy pants word for 'flared', so 'skinny jeans' is just a euphemism for 'denim leggings', a style that didn't even make it in the eighties.

But thanks to Kate Moss looking good in them (see *Moss, Kate, and how she ruined your wardrobe*) and a simple desire for a break from bootcut, skinny jeans were as ubiquitous as James Blunt for some time. But just because something has the word 'skinny' in the name does not mean it will actually make you skinny. If anything, you could see it as operating like an 18 certificate on a film in that it describes the only people who are advised to partake.

Men, for one, seem to understand this and so the only ones you ever see wearing skinny jeans are either musicians who subsist on a diet of opium and groupies, or half-starved fashion students. Women, however, are a more optimistic, or maybe just more self-confident, breed and happily squeeze themselves into the tightest denim leggings they can find.

Some find this blatant show of female curvature aesthetically upsetting. Yeah, well, some people apparently still take Tom Cruise seriously – what can you do about it? The real problem with skinny jeans is that they quietly ushered in their inevitable descendent, leggings, the non-denim kind. Because women had by now got used to wearing something super-tight on their legs and then a normal top, they continued to do the same, pairing leggings with a hip or waist-length top. Now, as lovely as a woman's anatomy is, there is no need for the general public to be on intimate terms with her gusset. It was certainly an interesting spin on the eighties look, but there are some times when you have to ask yourself whether there might be a reason that this style didn't work in the decade in which it originated.

Like bootcut, the hipster element was also ripe for a fall from grace due to its similar ubiquity, and so in 2005 and 2006 various brands dabbled with high-waisted styles, pish-tushing aside any complaints that this would remind people of how unflattering jeans once were. The thing about high-waisted is that although it will make you look thinner from the back because it pinches in your waist and holds in muffin toppage – a common problem with hipster jeans – it's generally not quite the same story from the front and sides because all the flesh that's being pinched in will be forced downwards to your stomach, giving you a denim pregnant bump. This can be quite useful on which to rest things like mugs of tea, but some people might feel this isn't sufficient compensation.

All of these issues illustrate why one should never pay attention to trends when it comes to trousers. Trends are there to allow customers to skip gaily through the fields of novelty and dabble with different looks, like small children let loose in the dress-up cupboard. I'm afraid trousers are just too serious a matter to be treated so frivolously. Because they hug and emphasize particular parts of one's anatomy it is very easy to look terrible in them or, more importantly, just to feel uncomfortable in them. For example, a woman with a tiny waist but wide bum is just going to feel awkward in hipsters simply because her trousers will keep slipping southwards, whereas if she opted for high-waisted she would get through the day with nary a care. No one style suits everyone and anyone who tells you anything different is trying to sell you something.

Jeans colours have gone through a similar 'new and improved' to 'ironic and retro' trajectory. At first, it was the most flattering shade, dark blue, but this quickly became dull and, with the emergence of the phenomenally successful Seven jeans, this then moved to lighter blue, to faded grey to black to, most improbably of all, white. Well, at least Johnny Borrell is happy. A crucial consideration in all of my fashion decisions.

Feathering and bleaching became popular design tweaks, each more annoying than the other. The point of these were to make the jeans look 'worn in', though why anyone thought adding some creased white lines around the crotch area would add appeal to anything is beyond me. Feathering basically looks like your geriatric merkin has slipped out of place or that you have drawn on some helpful arrows pointing the, um, way. As for fading, the reason jeans fade is because the denim wears down from being stretched over your body. Considering today's obsession with thinness – reflected, indeed, by the fact that most jeans are predicated on making the wearer look thinner – it's an odd concept that someone would want to buy jeans that look like they have been worn down from trying to rein in your heft. Moreover, the fading is always over the front of the legs and the bum, precisely the areas that work better with darker colours, not giant bleach spots acting like magnifying spotlights.

By all means, jeans needed some improving from their hideous days of yore. But it was when manufacturers started making solemn statements about light blue being this year's faded grey and knocking out limited edition crystal-studded £300 jeans that the denim industry jumped the shark. The whole reason jeans suddenly became so popular is because retailers learned how to make them look good. So to then start knocking out high-waisted versions in white does suggest that sight of the original appeal has been well and truly lost. It's not just retailers who are to blame but customers, too: once something becomes too popular we get bored. So to stay ahead you have to then move on to a previously untapped style. Yet the reason that style – white jeans, say – has not been seized yet by the masses is because it's not all that hot. Thus, in a scenario that recalls the film *Sophie's Choice*, you have to choose sometimes between looking fashionable and looking good. Your decision, but just ask yourself what you'd rather spend money on – impressing the overgrown kids in a bar in Hoxton or looking so fabulous you briefly consider having sex with your reflection in the bathroom mirror. No wonder so many people began to opt out and ran into the simpler embrace of shorts with tights and, sigh, leggings.

Jewellery, *and when fashion just gets obnoxious*

*L*ike fur, you can just about see the appeal of super expensive jewellery: it's shiny and twinkly and occasionally sort of pretty – yet so are fairy lights, but it doesn't mean you're going to spend £50,000 on them. There is absolutely no point to real jewellery except to show off how rich you are and to distract thieves from the rest of us poor folk when they're looking for someone on the streets to rob. Your only excuse would be if you were living in some soon-to-be-toppled economy and had to convert your remaining life savings into something that wouldn't be worthless by tomorrow. Seeing as few readers, I imagine, are currently living in early twentieth-century Russia, that argument holds little sway round here. You know the facts: it's offensively expensive, the gems are often unearthed through distastefully unethical methods involving small children and underground caves and if you don't feel a sense of disgust at wearing something around your neck that costs more than many people's house down payments then it might be time to do a little bit of soul searching. Wedding rings – fine; earrings to celebrate something like a tenth anniversary – fine; flashy jewellery for the sake of looking good at the latest charity dinner for whatever this month's trendy benefit is – not cool. Just give the money you spent on that stupid brooch that looks like you dribbled on your lapel to the charity, you daft woman, you.

All too often women think that if they're going to get the jewellery out, they may as well go for the whole hog. This then results in what is known as the Statement Piece. Think oversized clanging earrings, think hideous brooches, think whacking great necklace dangling down a woman's cleavage.

There are several problems with statement jewellery. First, it does precisely what it says on the tin – it makes a statement – and that statement tends to be that this oversized brooch in the shape of a bunch of gladioli is all you have to offer to the fashion conversation today. Moreover, it suggests that you are very proud of this piece, and you might want to think twice before saying that about a gladioli brooch. And finally, because you're metaphorically and possibly literally shoving it in people's faces, everyone will, if only out of politeness, comment on it throughout the day and you will have to trot out the story about how your grandmother left it to you in her will or whatever at least fifteen times, depending on how popular you are and how polite your friends are, until the sound of your own voice will make you want to rip that pin out of your lapel and stab it in your own vocal chords. And speaking of politeness, here's a handy hint: if you hear the phrase, usually uttered in a tone best described as 'tremulous', 'Oooh, what an extraordinary pin, wherever did you get it from?' this should not be taken as a compliment but rather a decorous euphemism. And if you hear it more than three times in twenty-four hours, ditch the pin.

But to quote the name of an old seventies book from this author's childhood – *Jewellery Can Be Fun!* And, in fact, that's when it's at its best – being fun and not all po-faced and ostentatious. Moreover, if it's a half-decent party you are guaranteed to lose at least one piece of jewellery so it just makes better sense to get, say, a £15 necklace in the shape of a chunky heart than a £115,000 pink diamond ring. *Sex and the City* was quite the master at showing how a woman can take pleasure in jewellery without it descending into something either offensive or clownish, with pieces such as Carrie's multi-strands of fake pearls and chunky bracelets. (The nameplate necklace, however, went just a touch too far. Who goes around flaunting their name in a big city, anyway? Girlfriend, do you want to be harassed on public transport?) This ties in with the recent popularity of charm bracelets and long earrings, which are certainly a lot more fun than boring Sloaney studs; oversized fake cocktail rings work with both jeans and T-shirts or party outfits and cost at most £10; long swinging strands of necklaces can look good, but you have to be flat-chested as otherwise they look like a geographical chart of a local hilly area. Brooches, though, are completely pointless: in what way does sticking some gimmicky little image on your lapel add to an outfit? Oversized hoop earrings had their moment until everyone realized that having one's lobes dragged down by the weight of these hoops or, worse, ripped downwards when your fingers got caught whilst doing a flirtatious hair flick really did not help a lady's mood on a night out. If you want a simple analogy, think of it like this: accessories are the sprinkles on a cake, there to improve, not form, the whole meal. They are not essential and, when done badly, definitely an oversweetened detriment. But when employed with a sage and delicate hand they make the difference between generic blandness and decorative indulgence.

Lagerfeld, Karl, *and why he's so brilliant*

*T*here are many reasons to love Karl Lagerfeld, but number one has got to be because – and this is meant in truly the best, most respectful of ways – he is such a fantastic bitch. His *mots*, some *bons* but more usually downright *mauvais*, are infamous, not just because of their perceptive accuracy, but the way he says them with a guileless expression as if he thinks he's saying something ever so supportive when in fact he may as well be carving out your heart with a spoon.

When Chanel dropped Kate Moss after the cocaine 'shock' scandal, only then to realize that, actually, the public wasn't quite as hypocritical as the media and therefore wanted her back, Lagerfeld praised how, 'Kate Moss has a lot of courage in the way she throws her life away in a very dangerous way, but that makes her so touching.' This is him being nice, by the way. Most famously, when Chloé hired Stella McCartney to take over as the brand's creative director, Lagerfeld said, calm as you like, 'I guess they wanted a name. Unfortunately they chose one in music, not fashion.'

Yet, incredibly, despite the bitchiness, Lagerfeld has managed to construct the most extraordinary self-image of being an ascetic intellectual: someone who scorns fashion fripperies to go home and read Proust in Aramaic before whipping off another thirty drawings for his next collection, rereading the whole of Emily Dickinson and then putting his priceless art collection in chronological order. And how do we know he does this? Because he constantly tells us. As self-branding methods go, it's not the most subtle. He talks loudly of how he hates most people (fair enough), has never taken drugs (probably true) and has no interest in sex (who knows? Who wants to?). Even though almost all autobiographical details he has ever uttered have proved to be total baloney, from his aristocratic German childhood oddly untouched by the war to whether or not he's ever been in love, the view of Lagerfeld as some sexless, inhuman genius still seems to be the generally accepted one. Recently, a German tabloid managed to confront him with alleged proof of his wariness of a concept called the truth by unearthing his birth certificate showing that Lagerfeld is actually a few years older than he had always claimed. Lagerfeld, proving that he does have previously denied cojones, responded by saying he would never reply to such 'trash'. This coming from a man who once dubbed Lindsay Lohan 'an icon' really is something.

His physical appearance also merits commendation. Once he was a ponytailed butterball who hid behind a fan to 'block out other people's bad breath'. But then one morning he decided he didn't like that look so much any more. Instead, he wanted to wear trousers made by his former tango dancing partner (and that is not, all parties insist, a euphemism), Hedi Slimane, then the creative director of Dior Homme. And so, on a diet he claims consisted primarily of cactus juice, this sixty- to seventy-something managed to lose over 80 pounds. Now he looks like a scary-looking sixteenth-century German courtier, just as I presume he intended.

Another reason is that, rather sweetly, the only time he makes good clothes is when he makes them in someone else's name. Lagerfeld's clothes for Chloé back in the day? Adorable, beautiful, splendid. His clothes for Chanel? Iconic, unbeatable, up there with the best in the world. His clothes for Fendi? Well, they're great if you like that skinned-chinchilla-coat look, which, apparently, a lot of people do. His clothes for his own imaginatively named label, Lagerfeld? You didn't even know they existed, did you? And what must really grate is that Lagerfeld subscribes to the Donatella Versace approach to fashion, making the designer the muse for the collection. Thus, should you accidentally find yourself at a Karl Lagerfeld fashion show you will more likely than not be confronted with a parade of thirty models all looking exactly like Lagerfeld, with slicked back hair and scary *Matrix*-like suits. When a sixty- (or seventy-) something-year-old German designer is able to make an eighteen-year-old girl from San Francisco look like him you know you are dealing with a serious talent. Sadly, few people actually want to look like a pensionable German designer. Lagerfeld, of course, claims not to give a stuff.

His clothes for Chanel in particular really are fantastic. They manage to stay on just the right side of pastiche so that they are recognizably Chanel without looking like you're en route to a costume party. They keep the original Chanel appeal – ladylike but girlish, a little bit cool, but very proper – but make them modern, such as delicate dresses mixed with biker boots, or piles of charm necklaces over a tweed jacket. It is hard to think of many other designers who can appeal to Sofia Coppola, Paris Hilton and Lauren Bacall in a single collection. Perhaps the only other one who can do this is Marc Jacobs (see *Jacobs, Marc, genius or what?*) who has publicly stated that his dream gig would be to take over at Chanel only for Lagerfeld to turn around and publicly state, more or less, that Jacobs could go boil his head.

Lagerfeld treats everything as a costume. He has adopted some weird public persona, maybe because he quite likes it, but almost certainly because he knew that such extremism would bring him fame and that is often the best advertisement for the brand. If he was really so private, we wouldn't know about it; if he was actually such an elitist intellectual snob, he wouldn't bring Lindsay Lohan as his date to a fashion dinner. Everything is about creating a perfectly constructed image, whether it be determinedly sidestepping the specifics of his personal life or living on cactus juice, so no wonder he flounders when it comes to designing his own collection. For this reason, he is the perfect designer for these image-obsessed days. Though if he ever heard this kind of psychoanalysis, he would probably tell me to choke on it. And, Karl, I'd love you even more for that.

Late, *fashionable and just rude*

$\mathscr{I}$ t is unfortunate that the word 'late' has somehow adopted the frequent prefix of 'fashionable', thereby fixing and perpetuating the idea in people's collective minds that it is elegant to keep people waiting. It is not. It is annoying and is yet another example of the irritating teenage mentality that pervades many areas of the fashion industry. Legends abound of the degrees of lateness practised by some of the industry's luminaries, the most famous probably being that of a notoriously time-phobic supermodel who once allegedly turned up dead on the appointed hour for a fashion shoot, albeit three days later than she was expected.

The fashion industry is built on the creation of false, glamorous images and when a person is late they are insinuating that they lead such a glamorous, busy life, jetting from P. Diddy in Malibu to Tom Ford in London, frankly you are lucky to get them at all, forty-five minutes late being neither here nor there. Thus, it is a very handy kind of self-advertisement, albeit one that will make most people hate you.

And the truth is, most fashion people do know this. They do know that turning up to meetings late is perhaps not the most professional way to behave and, in fact, no way to run a business. Thus, the dirty truth is that – shhhh! – most fashion people aren't late at all. Yes, it's true: designers don't tend to turn up half an hour late to interviews with journalists, and PRs are generally bang on time for those crucial expenses lunches with editors. But this is something people like to keep quiet about as it's just not very cool and so the only time they all are late is when everyone's on mass show to one another, i.e. at fashion shows and parties. Tellingly, the one person who is never late to either of these crucial events is Anna Wintour, who is always to be found perched in the front row dead on time at the shows, even though she knows she will have to spend at least the next hour staring blankly ahead from behind her sunglasses without even a newspaper to help her wile away the time (props to alleviate boredom are, it seems, somehow even less cool than being on time). As I said, this is telling because it proves that this lateness malarkey really is just about convincing everyone of your importance and if there is one person in this industry who does not need to bother to do this it is Wintour. It is somehow even more telling that being on time is possibly the one trend that Wintour has not been able to convince her followers to adopt. Yeah, well, we are talking about looking cool here and even Anna's powers can only extend so far.

Layering, *the whats and the hows of*

*T*he line between stylishly layered and appearing residentially challenged is on the slender side. But then, the line between the patron saint of layering, Kurt Cobain, and resembling a homeless man wasn't exactly fat either.

Matters aren't helped by fashion shoots involving models dashing around country piles wearing all manner of silk slip dresses and heavy tweed coats and anoraks that purport to show how glamorous layering can be but, in fact, to the untrained eye, look more like documentary footage from a 1930s lunatic asylum.

Fashion magazines love the layering look because it appears so devil-may-care in that uniquely aristo way and they can get something from every single advertiser into one shoot. Designers love it because it makes people think that instead of buying just one jumper they should buy three, an oversized blouse, a skirt and maybe those extra-thick socks too. Whether either of these factors were what Kurt intended from his fashion legacy is unknown, but it is not for us to fathom the mind of a genius.

Layering is simply a way to stay warm whilst wearing whatever the heck you want. Thus, long-sleeved shirts can go under summer dresses and woolly tights work surprisingly well under delicate party dresses. A pretty vest over a warm top is just about acceptable, but prepare yourself to be asked by your father whether you're off to battle in your new suit of armour – hilarious!

This is what a trend should do: show how certain clothes can be worn in ways you never thought of before. It should not be about brainwashing people into wearing something so laughably stupid that they spend the rest of their lives tracking down photos of themselves from that era in order to destroy them.

For boys, the situation is subtly different, simply because they have a longer and not entirely noble layering tradition which has therefore picked up all manner of associations. The faux stoner-like appearance of the look somewhat grates as the wearer is trying to go for a laidback California dude effect when in fact he is clearly as image conscious as the next boy band lead singer, seeing as piling a T-shirt on top of a long-sleeved top is not a dressing ritual that tends to come naturally. Unless, of course, he is stoned, which at least explains why he doesn't seem to have washed either of the tops since 1998.

Even more wearying is a single, articulated garment made to give a double-layered effect. Like pre-ripped jeans, pre-washed trousers or pre-bleached T-shirts, this is the worst kind of lazy artificiality, up there with pre-chipped, 'antique' wooden furniture from a department store or a 'home-made' Waitrose chocolate cake. This is not to say that we should all return to making our own bread or whatever because we all know that ready-made is generally a lot better – well, a lot easier, anyway, which, to some of us, amounts to the same thing. But rather, that if you are going to embrace the artificial, at least acknowledge what you're doing as opposed to kidding yourself that you're really communing with nature in your Cath Kidston tent. And if you really are too lazy to layer two shirts on top of one another yourself, well, then, maybe that is God's way of telling you you shouldn't bother anyway.

Leather jackets, *and the delusion of the middle-aged man*

*A*h, Bruce Springsteen, Paul Weller and Joe Strummer. The havoc that you have wreaked! You thought you were expressing the primal male psyche; in fact, you provided the fashion template for men to express that beneath that button down shirt from the M & S Blue Harbour Range beats the heart of a young tiger whose legs are metaphorically slung across a motorcycle on Route 66 even if, in reality, they are squeezed inside a Volvo Accord on the school run.

Just as dressing in skinny jeans has the opposite effect of making them look skinny on most people, so dressing in clothes from one's youth won't make you look like you are still in your youth. In fact, the yawning gap between seventeen and fifty-five visibly opens up in the contrast between the leather neckline and the gravity-embracing jowls. We should all salute the power of fashion and all that, but a leather jacket is no Tardis. Just get yourself a decent woollen jacket or even a smart wool or tweed coat and have done with it. It's a little like when celebrities claim, despite all visible evidence that this is unlikely, that they are twenty-six: contrary to widespread belief, the general public is not quite so stupid, nodding their heads bovinishly and repeating like a brainwashed cult as one, 'Twenty-six, yes, mistress, you are twenty-six . . .' Instead, those who aren't raising their eyebrows in awe at the audacity of the celebrity's pathetic ploy will merely muse on how old the celebrity looks for her age and how badly she seems to be ageing, poor thing. Claiming to be a twenty-six-year-old won't make you look like you're twenty-six, just as forcing yourself into a pair of size 10 trousers won't make you look like a size 10 and just as dressing like Bruce won't fool people into thinking you were, indeed, born to run, in your Volvo Accord, if need be.

Limits, age, *and what's (allegedly) acceptable when*

*A*longside 'the new elegance' and 'what's hot now' the most popular fashion magazine coverline is 'how to look fabulous at every age'. It is notable how this idea is invariably touted as a novel revelation: my God, can you actually imagine a woman looking good past the age of thirty-five?

And no surprise, really. Designers are frequently accused of taking a harder line against age than the folk in *Logan's Run*. In truth, though, designers have a good amount of respect for a more mature vintage, if only because they tend to comprise a large proportion of their customer base.

Yet this rarely comes across in the magazines because the clothes, no matter which age group they're aimed at, are invariably modelled by sunken-cheeked pubescents. It's difficult to trust these publications to know what looks good on a sixty-five year old seeing as they insist on dressing eighteen year olds in clothes made for someone who's fifty.

Many rules get bandied around about what's acceptable in which decade of our fashion lives, all of which can be summed up as: the older you are, the less of you we want to see. Some people in the west might reel back in horror at the Muslim tradition of making women wear burkhas to hide their unacceptable femininity, but such smugness seems misplaced if we do the same thing, albeit slightly later in life and using more expensive labels.

The biggest concern of these features is to teach women what is 'appropriate' for their age, and, over the age of forty, showing any inch of skin at all is definitely 'inappropriate' because someone, somewhere, might see skin that isn't entirely smooth. The horror, the horror!

Of course, as one gets older one's body changes and what once looked cute might start to merit a slightly different adjective. But the reason some women dress too young for their age is because they understandably fear being dismissed and ignored by the current anti over thirty-five culture. It seems unlikely that counselling them to wear blazers with brass buttons and carrying about strange handbags in the shape of small animals will make them feel better or assuage their fears about the future.

In truth, the real fault in dressing too young for your age is not the aesthetic distress it might cause to onlookers, but that it suggests you have somehow failed to learn certain lessons along the years. Only the very young, for example, are (just about) tolerated for wearing T-shirts with silly slogans, simply because their brains are still soft and have yet to soak in the lesson that writing across one's chest is not quite the last word in chic. The twenties and early thirties are a hard time of life, when one begins to realize that Saturday night is no longer synonymous with getting smashed out of your brain, but rather dithering over a Nigella Lawson cookbook while your friends sit in the living room talking about things like 'mortgages' and 'childcare'. No wonder these traumatized souls so frequently try to block out the roar of encroaching maturity by buying overpriced accessories, and hide their fearful selves beneath trends like layering and volume. By the time a lady is in her forties, she is beginning to emerge from this cocoon of trend dabbling and show herself to be the butterfly she always was, now aware of what suits her personally and what doesn't. Once she reaches her fifties she knows that wearing high heels all day long is actually a total faff and a woman in wide-legged trousers and flats is actually a far better proposition than those magazines ever let on, particularly when paired with a cool short-sleeved blouse. And by the time she gets into her sixties, well, it would be downright insulting for me to make any suggestions seeing as she now is far too wise and experienced to need any guidance, having long since found the personal style that suits her.

This issue of personal style is utterly jettisoned by these age features. Just as horoscopes seem to believe that a twelfth of the population will all be making a journey that day simply because they were born in May, so these features operate on the idea that whole age groups have exactly the same personal tastes, figures and forms of self-expression. Maybe some Taureans are going on a long voyage that day, and maybe some sixty-somethings genuinely do long for an Armani trouser suit. But I'd wager a lot aren't and don't.

These magazines reply that, actually, they're giving women confidence because they show how one can look good as one gets older despite the fact that, um, they've been saying the opposite for the rest of the year. And this is a reasonable argument if it didn't have a touch of the brainwashing cult leader to it: 'Come, follow our way and only our way. Never mind your own personal inclinations, you'll be much happier with us . . .' As I said, some women do dress too young for their age to no one's benefit, but there is a world of alternatives between a pink ruffled party dress and a boring blue trouser suit.

And to be honest, if a woman manages to get to the unimaginably ancient age of, say, fifty-two without having been bludgeoned into hermit-hood or turned into a raving fanatic by the anti-age bias of the modern world, well, I'd say she has more than earned the right to wear a sleeveless top if she darn well wishes.

Lingerie, *and the importance or otherwise of an audience*

When Andrea Dworkin was out there fighting for women to take control of their bodies and their sexuality, she probably didn't consider how brilliantly this would relate to the lingerie business. Nor was it probably her secret life ambition to see her name in a fashion book in a section about silky knickers. But as Dworkin no doubt mused somewhere, we still live in an era when a woman's destiny is still not wholly in her power.

Once sexy lingerie was all about the audience, with the wearer forced to truss herself up in nasty itchy stuff that probably had a detachable bunny tail. But then a nice couple called Joe Corre and Serena Rees came up with the idea that looking sexy and feeling uncomfortable and like a traitor to the feminist cause need not be quite so closely aligned. Lo, Agent Provocateur was born, teaching the world that 'sexy lingerie' wasn't French for 'red and scratchy'. This was shortly followed by Myla, Damaris and the downright brilliant M & S Salon Rose range and the store's own brand fantastic boy shorts selection.

The thing is, while it is always nice to be appreciated, lingerie should be about making the wearer feel good in herself. Forget about G-strings, which are horrible and make no woman feel sexy unless sexy has somehow become a synonym for 'two molars, mid-floss' (see *G-strings, and the female lie*). It is just very cheering to know that you have pretty little satin things with bits of frills here and there beneath your crumpled suit during another dull day in the office.

Some women say they find it depressing to wear nice lingerie if they know there will be no audience appreciation. Yeah, well, some women actually watched *Ally McBeal* instead of dismissing it for being the misogynistic twaddle it was. To see lingerie as something purely for a spectator is to forget the point of fashion – to make yourself feel good – and play right into the hands of all those who try to make women feel bad about themselves by saying that fashion is purely about shallow vanity and all of you silly girls should just get back into your frumpy old sack dresses and in the kitchen where you belong. And so, as Andrea would no doubt say if she were still here, go on, ladies – fight against these nasty women haters by going out there and buying some silk knickers! Yeah! Right on!

Logos, *the bleating of the insecure*

ne might have thought that it would be difficult to put a price on that happy inner glow one gets from a sense of validation. Oh foolish naivety! It's an easy 150 per cent mark-up, madam, and have a nice day. That is what designer logos do: they are a reassuring pat on the head to those who are so devoid of any confidence in their own taste that they rely on the name of someone who they've never met, and probably wouldn't even like, to be slapped on their clothes and accessories to make them feel that they have made a good purchase. This also means that the man or woman sporting the logo has such low expectations of their fellow human creatures that they expect them, too, to be impressed by this voluntary human billboard look, which, when you think about it, is kind of insulting. Really, it's a wonder that fashion companies spend billions of dollars every year on magazine and magazine advertising when so many customers out there are happy to pay them to wander around town on a daily basis, serving the same purpose.

Louis Vuitton must be the prime culprit on this score, not because this brand necessarily slaps its name about more than anyone else (Chanel, Dior and Armani could easily give it a run for its money, and that's not even mentioning Burberry's check, Missoni's stripes or Pucci's swirls, which serve pretty much the same purpose as a logo), but because it has milked so much more out of this wheeze. Louis Vuitton luggage and handbags are little more than well-made but irrefutably dull brown suitcases. Yet because of the repeated burnished tan LV motif adorning the hardware they not only cost more than most pieces of furniture, but they have somehow become an indisputable symbol of French chic. Vuitton's creative director, Marc Jacobs, has enjoyed huge success by having a bit of fun with this logo veneration thing, and by 'fun' I mean making them multi-coloured, decorating them with Japanese cartoon flowers and turning them into graffiti tags. Some might describe this as ironic; others might see it as proof that all the guff about Louis Vuitton has less to do with the logo's oft-cited 'timeless appeal' and rather more to do with the seemingly timeless desire to flaunt designer names.

I'm all for people getting credit where credit's due and one could say that a designer logo works in the same way as credits at the end of the film, letting admiring or otherwise onlookers know who's responsible for the creative endeavour in question. Yet film credits tend to come quietly at the end of the movie; they aren't splattered across the film itself.

Once you have a name that is deemed worthy of becoming a logo, you have metaphorically headed down to City Hall and drawn yourself up a licence to print cash. Stick it on a plastic compact that probably cost about seven pence to manufacture and flog the silly thing for twenty quid; slosh it across the backs of jeans, bikinis and even ski equipment if you like and multiply the retail price tags by at least three. Ah, there's nothing like being in the fresh alpine air, looking down at one's feet and seeing the reassuring double C of the Chanel logo on your skis to really make you feel like you are connecting with nature.

Most of all, logos reek of the worst kind of fashion victimhood. They suggest the following mentality: 'Gosh, this dress is kinda hideous, isn't it? Oh, wait a minute, it says Lacroix across the front so it must be OK.' 'So it must be OK' – is there any other phrase in the English language that smacks so strongly of a recent lobotomy and the mindless following of others' opinions, whether in the fashion context or elsewhere? Logos reduce fashion itself to the most cynical of clichés – that it is about pointless displays of conspicuous wealth as opposed to making one feel genuinely good about oneself. If you can only justify the purchase of something by the fact someone else's name is written across it as opposed to, say, its simple beauty, then it's probably safe to say that it is not a purchase worth making. Heck, you may as well just buy a ten-pence name tag from WH Smith, write the designer's name on that and pin it to yourself. Good to go, girlfriend!

Now a whole new level of snobbery has affixed itself to fashion labels. In the late nineties/early twenty-first century (sorry, can't be dealing with that 'noughties' lark again), designer logos were quite the thing, with much guff written about 'logomania' and what have you. And then – gasp – people who didn't go to St Kitts every April dared to try to get in on the act and started sporting designer logos about their person. This then led to one of the uglier episodes so far this century in British pop culture, the coinage of 'chav fashion' which basically amounted to mockery of anyone who was Not Quite Our Class, Dear wearing designer logo clothes. How *dare* these mucky sorts try to muscle in on fashion's codified system? Shouldn't there be, like, a test one has to take before being allowed to buy a Chanel Cambon handbag?

Certainly what has been dubbed 'chav chic' has its decided aesthetic downsides. But no more than designer logos do as a whole anyway. So it seems a bit rich for Louis Vuitton, say, to spend millions on an advertising campaign featuring Uma Thurman lovingly stroking an LV'd-up bag, only then to get a bit antsy when a footballer's fiancée is photographed displaying a similar fondness for those initials. Get back in your place, you Scouse madam! (But, er, thanks for the thousand quid.)

Logos more than any other style statement are glaringly dependent on context, which is why designers get all in a fluster when the 'wrong sort' sport them. When an acceptably aspirational A-lister flaunts them they, the general mentality goes, look rich and glamorous. But when someone a little lower down the celebrity alphabet does, logos are shown up for what they are: the bleating of the insecure, and a demonstration of desperation for acceptance by the chronically shallow. In this sense, they are a useful reminder of how thumpingly useless it is to look to fashion icons for style guidance (see *Celebrities, and when bad ones happen to good fashion*). In all other respects, they are the detritus of a look that should have faded out with Ivana Trump's heyday.

Low slung belts, *the point thereof*

*N*ot a lot, one would have thought. And one would be right. Some people, bless their souls, think that a belt is something with which to hold your trousers up. They are still mentally operating in the Pre Sienna era, that time before a blonde west Londoner showed how putting on an oversized belt made one look thinner (look, I'm so thin even my belt can't fit around my childlike hips!), cooler (I am just so busy, dashing between meeting my A-list boyfriend and my private plane to Marrakech that I don't even have time to put my belt on properly. Sorry!) and pleasingly eco-aware, thanks to its vaguely hippy connotations, it being very un-ecologically friendly to buy a belt that fits properly as opposed to wearing one of your dad's old ones.

To be fair, a low slung belt can help to control the potential maternity sack look of that new tunic dress you bought from Gap by gently reigning in the volume, whereas a normal belt would cinch around your waist and stomach, thereby divesting the tunic of its main appeal – that you can eat as much as you like in it without looking like a snake digesting a rabbit. Plus it does give an interesting insight into what it must feel like to be a teenage boy who insists on wearing his jeans halfway down around his upper thighs (answer: quite stupid, and a little incapacitated), and it's always nice to show a little empathy with the lower forms of life. But in all other instances, it is gratingly superfluous.

Magazines, *fashion, and women's masochistic love thereof*

The argument that fashion quite simply makes women feel bad about themselves can be disproved by one little number: 220,000. That's how many copies of *Vogue* are sold in this country every month. And while a certain portion of those readers may well comprise whip wielders and bondage queens, I'd be surprised if they accounted for the total.

The idea that women are helpless little victims, meekly buying *In Style* every month in order to receive their monthly flagellation has the suspicious stench of a ready-made theory cooked up by lazy newspaper columnists with a wordcount to fill and a deadline to meet.

For a start, we now live in an era when most of us dose ourselves up with more drugs at the first hint of a cold than Syd Barrett got through in a month, buy pre-chopped vegetables to save a whole two minutes' cooking time and do a large part of our shopping over the internet thereby brilliantly avoiding inconveniences such as standing up and walking. So the idea that women would go out of their way to find something to make life hard for themselves doesn't really have the smack of likelihood to it. The truth is, women buy fashion magazines because they like them.

Fashion magazines full of pretty girls wearing expensive clothes and living ever so glamorous lives should make you feel no worse about yourself than, say, some high octane blockbuster film full of, ahem, pretty girls wearing expensive clothes and living their own glamorous, exciting, multi-orgasmic lives, yet I have yet to hear Harvey Weinstein being taken to account for women's mental health issues in the way Anna Wintour is. Magazines, like movies, are there to provide you with a few hours of fun fantasy, that's why women buy them. If they were templates for reality they'd be called life magazines, not fashion magazines, and, seeing as we can all see reality every day for free, they'd probably have a much lower circulation.

If a woman is already prone to self-hatred issues then, yes, she will find a fair amount of fodder to nurture those tendencies in a fashion magazine, just as she would down her local Odeon. For the majority, sure, maybe there is some initial self-dissatisfaction at first when looking at pages of hipless women, overpriced dresses and holidays that are about as close to most people's reality as a day in the life of James Bond. But this is swiftly dissipated by the sheer fun of looking at the clothes, picking out the ones you'd buy in a parallel universe and finding similar versions in Topshop, and reading another article about why high hems are back this season written with the kind of gravity usually reserved for think tank reports. Women, by and large, are not small children who are incapable of distinguishing between fantasy and reality, and, even if one were to spend five years solid reading a fashion magazine, there is no guarantee that she would come away thinking that jutting bones and piano key ribs are the norm. She might have a slightly odd perception of what constitutes good value for money when it comes to clothes, but that's a different issue.

You want to know why women buy fashion magazines? Because sometimes it's nice to read something that is just for us. Not about our kids, not about our boyfriends and how to 'please' the lazy sods, not about our jobs, or our parents, or about any worthwhile cultural pursuits or political causes even though we know we should understand better, but 100 per cent totally about us. Not us in reality, of course, but us in a fantasy world, where we do get fresh sea salt scrubs in Bali every 'spring break', whatever that is, and actually do change our entire wardrobe every six months. It's a land where your Tesco bag never splits in the middle of the street introducing the world to your banana custard addiction and where boyfriends never dump you and where you never spend another night in watching another day in the life of *Holby City*. We just want lots of lovely pictures of things we could wear in a different planetary system and interviews with people who 'divide their time' between multiple continents.

Moreover, fashion magazines are decidedly upbeat affairs due to an inability to criticize anything because of the looming black cloud of advertisers (see *Advertising, how it spins the fashion axis*). They are certainly far more cheerful than the weekly gossip magazines that have sprouted like fungi in the past five years. These are almost entirely comprised of allegedly bad photos of female celebrities who have dared to be mid-blink when the shutter clicked or left the house in something other than Dior couture, the shameless slatterns. These magazines like to claim that bringing celebrities down a peg makes women feel better, when, really, their message is that a woman must never blink when a camera's in the room as even Uma Thurman gets scolded about this.

In the land of the fashion magazine, however, everyone is fabulous and no one ever does anything wrong. Admittedly, the increasingly prevalent interviews with eighteen-year-old models can be a bit of a downer, purely due to their uniformity: favourite food – sushi; favourite pastime – surfing, sure as eggs, every time. Still, it's nice to have something you can rely on in this cold world of ours.

And even if the magazine isn't up to snuff one month and doesn't provide you with the usual satisfaction, the knowledge that there are 220,000 other *Holby* escapists out there with you probably will.

Make-up, *the tears of a clown*

*L*ike high heels, make-up is one of those things that makes you simultaneously pity and envy the male of the species. Pity because one has to be occasionally grateful to the array of armoury at a lady's service there to make her look just that little bit better on days when her hotness quotient is not at its usual high level. But envy, too, because it is a bit of a pain to be expected to put this extensive armoury to use instead of just slinging oneself in the shower, spritzing on a bit of the Lynx effect and heading out on the town, confident that one has done about as much as one is reasonably expected to do.

There is something slightly odd about the idea of make-up anyway. With its emphasis on coloured eyelids, unnaturally heavy lashes, pink cheeks and big red lips one cannot help but trace a very obvious lineage between a gal's night-time look and that of a clown. Sure, slightly flushed cheeks and pinked lips might make one look a little nicer on washed-out days, even if, inevitably, some wisearse somewhere has propounded the theory that the appeal of this is that it makes a woman look, yes, mid-orgasm (see also *Heels, the highs, the lows and when fat is better than thin* for a similar cod theory that suggests socio-cultural theorists spend too many sweaty-palmed hours in the library). And we've all had cause to thank the little guy who invented concealer in our collective time.

Yes, make-up does make us look better, or what our view of 'better' is. Most of the time this means simply 'younger' (see *Anti-ageing*) or 'a little less tired', but without wishing to come across too ragingly militant here, perhaps we need to reconsider some of our concepts of beauty because there is some make-up that makes neither hide nor hair of sense. Coloured eyelids, anyone? Just who decided that neon-coloured eyelids were the surest way to a man's heart, or just a fast track to a party look in general? Curling eyelashes are, to be honest, just weird and eye pencil as a whole is an odd concept, at least to anyone who has a natural aversion to sticking a pencil into their eyeball, or giving themselves cat-like eyes with a marker pen. Lipliner is a no-win idea because either your lips have a naturally defined line already or, if it is slightly faded due to what is euphemistically referred to as 'feathering', also known as wrinkles, the liner will often emphasize this by falling into the, um, feathers, or whatever the accepted euphemistic term is. Lipgloss is great if you actively pursue the 'mouth slobberer' look and find trying to talk with strands of hair attached to your lips a challenge you wish to master one day. And don't even get me started on red fingernails. All right, fine, do: excellent if you want to look like some Agatha Christie murderer, blood dripping from your fingers. Once you ask yourself why some things are prized above others, veritable floodgates open that may, admittedly, say more about your own psyche than that of society's.

Anything that will give you what the beauty industry calls, with its endearing obliviousness to the concept of the oxymoron, a 'natural sparkle', is only permissible if you are still not legally allowed to buy alcohol or if you have somehow jumped in Marty McFly's Delorean and turned up in Studio 54, circa 1976.

Unless you are a burlesque dancer, make-up is generally there to make you look better, not make you look like you're wearing make-up. Hence 'the natural look' – a phrase that gets creakily wheeled out pretty much every month in every fashion magazine's beauty section – basically means a full face of make-up, but the lips perhaps a little more pink than full-on red and the eyelashes slightly longer and darker. 'The vamp look', on the other hand, is pleasingly honest in its description because, with its inevitable powdered face, pruned back eyebrows and crimson lips, it does encapsulate how most people imagine a vampire to look. No one is really sure what on earth the 'preppy' or 'English rose' looks really mean, other than, in both cases, an appreciation of flushed cheeks and perfect skin. I know, the novelty.

Manicures, pedicures *and the ever-rising bar of personal upkeep*

*L*et's blame Jennifer Aniston for this one. True, the woman has suffered quite a bit in recent times, but my unswayable pursuit of the truth forces me to point out the telling synchronicity between Aniston's glossed-up appearance on British TV and the mould-like sprouting of manicure, pedicure, eyebrow and now Botox bars on corners around the country.

Oh sure, there have been plenty of actresses before who could combine that lucrative double act of looking accessibly normal yet obviously extremely well-groomed. But none before did it at such a highly visible level as Aniston as she appeared in one of the most successful and, as viewers of E4 know all too well, most repeated TV series in the history of the universe. A comparison between the almost scruffy Aniston of the *Friends*' first series and the nigh-on unrecognizable one in the last provides an interesting lesson in just how much impact daily 'treatments', an expensive hair stylist and a personal yoga teacher can have on a woman's appearance and, by inevitable extension, professional success. And finally, she showed how, with just a bit of grooming, even a woman with naturally big hair and a face more cute than conventionally pretty might one day find herself up at the altar with Brad Pitt. That she then lost him to Angelina Jolie, a woman so well-groomed that she even managed to stave off hair frizz when marching through Namibia eight months pregnant and no doubt thinking of how to restore world peace, merely proves the point. But since Jolie looks like she recently landed on earth from the planet Terrifying Cyber Babe Clone while Aniston could easily be your friend from the office, it's the latter who has been the more influential on women's behaviour and their belief in their own aesthetic potential.

Less than a decade ago British women mocked what they saw as a purely and typically American obsession with this kind of grooming. My God, could you imagine, we'd marvel? All those nail bars on our cobbled British streets, taking the place of our noble eel and pie takeaways, our first edition Shakespeare bookshops, our sixteenth-century ye olde tea shoppes, or whatever other smug national stereotypes were wheeled out? Well, here we are, ten years on, veritably drowning in yoga centres, coffee 'bars' (sounds a bit trendier, presumably, than 'coffee shop', not to mention the continental glamour in referring to your waitress as 'a barista') and, yes, beauty treatment outlets.

There are several downsides to this development. First, due purely to availability, it is increasingly an expectation for women to make use of such venues. Where once a slick of Immac while watching '*Enders* did the trick, now a woman's pre-holiday preparations include spending a day going to her waxer, pedicurist, manicurist, eyebrow threader, hairdresser (for that crucial 'sun and sea proctector' treatment) and fake tanner. The sensation one feels when trying to coordinate all of the above with that funny little thing called 'a job' is called a panicure. True, you could call it a medicure, but that sounds a bit too like medical insurance, although that, too, has a certain kind of aptness as all this pressure combined with required energy schlepping from treatment to treatment could send a strong lady into ER.

It is one of those strange little facts that the fashion and beauty world spews in our faces from time to time: the only people who have time to master all of the above are those who don't have to work. Yet few would be able to shell out the £30 upwards necessary for each of the above (plus £100 for the hairdresser) without some kind of regular income. Thus, all this grooming malarkey has nothing to do with good style or even looking good: rather, it is simply another signifier, up there with vintage (see *Vintage*), of a life of indolent ease.

Masculinity, *and the clothes that challenge it*

*I*t is a shame but not in the least bit surprising that fashion has accrued girly or gay associations. To claim that pride in one's appearance is solely a feminine instinct, women being such silly and shallow creatures, whereas men are thinking far too many big thoughts to have time to look in the mirror, is entirely in keeping with a lot of the gender-based nonsense that still, incredibly, gets spouted in the twenty-first century. It is also quite patently wrong, as anyone who has ever seen a portrait of pretty much any male member of the upper classes from the nineteenth century and before knows.

Whereas women are allowed to spend their Saturdays trying on dresses with their friends without anyone questioning their sexual preferences, men, understandably jealous, can only retaliate by clinging on to the belief that taking an interest in one's appearance is a bit, y'know, gay. In point of fact, a man would have to have serious doubts about the strength of his heterosexual convictions if he feared they might be pushed over to the other side by trying on a jumper. This is what is known as irony.

And so men are forced to channel their perfectly human interest in fashion into more permissible vessels. Thus, they get pathetically excited over unbearably tedious things like ties, cufflinks and watches. Really, it's like seeing a dog having to make do with a table leg.

And just look at the tragic thrill aroused by any male celebrity who seems to take some kind of effort over their appearance. Russell Brand is the archetypal case in point, with men's magazines practically wetting their Calvin Kleins when he first emerged with his sparkly scarf even though the middle-aged ladies of Hampstead have been working that look for years. Pete Doherty is another prime example, having done nothing other than lie around, God knows where, wearing jeans two sizes too small and his grandad's trilby, and suddenly he is, and I quote, 'The most exciting thing to happen to men's style since the Rat Pack.' Well, at least they got the rat part right.

Frank Sinatra, Bryan Ferry, Jarvis Cocker – the men who make up the acceptable male-style-icon roster are a fairly predictable bunch being, respectively, a suit wearer, a tighter suit wearer and a velvet suit wearer. As Catholicism has shown us all, you try to crush a human tendency, the tendency will only pervert, and if a three-decade veneration of a man called Bryan isn't a sign of perversion, well, it's a weird old world we live in.

Even aside from fashion in general there are some garments that are seen as especial signs of an effeminate nature. Number one is pink but, really, if men would reclaim this colour the world would be much improved as it would be divested of its girlish associations and therefore not be used and abused in the manner it is now (see *Pink*). Second, tight T-shirts, but that's just because straight boys tend to fat when they're over thirty so they have to think of some excuse for covering the belly. Next up, waistcoats, as sported by the lovely Warren in *This Life* who was dressed by possibly the laziest wardrobe department this side of *The Matrix*. See also Simon Callow in *Four Weddings and a Funeral*. Again, this is foolish as waistcoats are rather nifty, they provide tummy coverage and, boys, you can have far more pattern fun here than you currently indulge yourselves in with your ties. With typical gaucheness, the once camp pieces that the straights have reclaimed for themselves are, inevitably, the worst: cropped combats, gelled hair, designer jeans and colourful button down shirts (see *Party shirts, the fun lovin' guy's staple*). It's like watching a woman diet all day and then binge herself stupid on Häagen-

Dazs when she gets home in the evening, stoically denying herself in one area only then to lose all self-control in the most misguided way as possible. Boys, boys, boys! Stop kidding yourselves and let your inner sartorial soul fly. Get yourself some proper trousers – not ones that are apologetically baggy or try-hard skinny – just normal, good trousers; a nice top from somewhere like John Smedley that suggests you might have a body under there somewhere and is in a not too garish colour; a proper haircut and some smart, plain shoes, such as decent brogues or trainers that don't look like they were designed for astronauts. A facial wouldn't go amiss either because pretending you don't have spots doesn't actually mean the rest of the world can't see them. It may not be the ever so manly pursuit of, I don't know, wrestling but honestly, you will find the results a lot more personally beneficial.

Menswear for women – *sexy subversion versus just a bit butch*

*T*he overwhelming personal objection to the idea that menswear for women is sexy is that it reflects and plays into men's beyond-parody fascination with lesbians. Now is not the time or place to go into just how unbelievably boring this malarkey is and how men are doing themselves absolutely no favours in confirming pretty much every demeaning cliché about their gender (only interested in women who aren't interested in them, the more tits the better, et cetera and so forth) by subscribing, tongues lolling, to this predictable stereotype. But one's silence on the matter is by no means an indication of tacit approval or, darn it, even resigned acceptance.

Anyway, yes, some menswear pieces do look quite nice on women. Good straight trousers, for example, or a leather biker jacket – general basics, in other words, as opposed to a full on tux affair which should only be attempted if you are going to a Dietrich revival party. Far better to take tips from the mens' market and then improve on them. Stella McCartney, for example, has made clever hay with transferring some of her Savile Row training into the womenswear market and knocking out men's white button down shirts cut for a woman's body and suit jackets so slick and narrow they make one look feminine and sexy as opposed to like a frumpy business woman who is too harried to buy clothes that fit properly. Jean Paul Gaultier, on the other hand, seems to find the idea of women dressing as men a concept that never fails to amuse, despite having been milking this one for two decades. But then, he also apparently believes that it's a bit of a wheeze for a French man to only ever sport a top with horizontal stripes so clearly he is a man with a rather courageous appreciation of the fashion cliché.

The least acceptable twist of this trend has been the recent development of young starlets wearing mens' clothes in an attempt to achieve a sexy post-coital look. Oversized men's shirts belted and worn with nothing other than a pair of black tights and Balenciaga boots; denim jackets at least three sizes too large for their twig-like shoulders; enormous men's jumpers over skinny jeans: all have been spotted on the awesome likes of the Olsen twins in recent years. Of course, part of the appeal of this look is that voluminous clothes emphasize their own bony fragility. But the sartorial reference to that always fashionable accessory – a boyfriend – can only be a boon, too, even if these girls look so undernourished that wearing a giant lumberjack shirt is probably the closest they've recently come to anything that can be described as post-coital. Still, if you can't live the dream, at least you can look the part, right, ladies?

Mittens, *and the enduring appeal of paedo chic*

*P*aedo chic is a state of mind, a fashion statement and a misguided path trodden by many celebrities and normal ladies
alike, surprisingly never learning from the errors of their forebears.
Many a pop star who will go unlibellously unmentioned has opted
for a style seemingly aimed at men who find women over the age of
sixteen a little bit scary. Did Natalie Imbruglia ever wear mittens in
a music video? Possibly not, but that is the sort of image that comes
to mind, and quite probably to that of mitten-wearing ladies, when
one thinks of this childish winter wear. Just as Imbruglia tends to
play on the little-girl-lost image in her videos, all big-eyed, narrow-
hipped and generally half undressed, so mittens evoke a kind of
sweet, childlike helplessness that, apparently, some women think is
a winner of a look.

Once you are over the age of eight there is just no excuse for
mittens. Aside from the Imbruglia factor, they turn your
hands into weird little paws so that you can't do
important things like write text messages or attend to your Marlboro
Light. This is what God gave
you opposable thumbs for, you
know.

Along with oversized buttons,
frilled socks, Mary Jane shoes,
heart-shaped sunglasses, skirts with petticoats
peeking out and anything with a pompom, mittens are part of what
can be referred to as, crudely if justly, paedo chic.

Paedo chic provides a salutary and aesthetically, morally and intellectually upsetting lesson to us all about the dangers of taking
youth veneration too far. While all women are trained from birth that
looking younger is always better, the usual definition of younger, i.e.

eighteen, seems to have somehow been mistranslated as being about four. It is the most extraordinary sight to see a grown woman in a cropped swingy little jacket with a frilled collar, some sort of A-line pink skirt and then little buckle-my-shoe footwear, looking for all the world as if she were en route to her own christening. Grayson Perry seems to be the style icon and the effect is not to any woman's benefit (and while we're here, why is that when transvestites say they want to 'dress as women' this tends to mean 'cabaret bar owners' or 'toddlers'? Never a simple LBD, or a good pair of jeans or even just a brilliant Topshop summer dress that everyone thinks you bought from Chloé – in other words, the best things about being a woman. Guys, you are seriously missing out.)

Paedo chic works in the same way as pink (see, yes, *Pink*) in that it provides a very reassuring sartorial symbol to the world that you are not to be taken seriously in the slightest. After all, you're just a cutesy wootsy little thing, a bit 'wacky', maybe, but, you know, not in a scary way, who likes nothing better in an evening than to go home, lie on your bed covered in cuddly toys and crank up the Dido.

Even if your appreciation of paedo chic really is based purely on aesthetics, ask yourself this: do you really want to hang around with someone who is attracted to a thirty-something dressed like a pre-pubescent? I mean, think of the potential for jealousy – no longer would you just have to keep an eye on him around other women at parties, but instead it would be every time you passed a school playground during the day. Oh the stress! And stress, as you know, is just terribly ageing.

Models

From Twiggy to Cindy to Kate to Gisele, one can trace the obsessions of each decade by looking at the models – respectively, stoned teenagers, aerobics, hard drugs, sex. Not, she hastily adds, that the aforementioned models necessarily partook in the listed activities, but that their looks perfectly reflected the fascinations of their eras.

For this reason, for all the fuss that newspapers make about the nefarious influence wielded by models on women's susceptible minds, models – possibly the most passive instruments of alleged control this side of Monica Lewinsky – are merely the reflection of the public's current insecurities and voyeuristic obsessions. Currently, judging from the number of underweight teenagers on the catwalks these days the current fascination is – no, you'll never guess – thinness.

Models have always been, and probably always will be, thin. But there is no question that they seem to have become thinner every year since the mid nineties. Everyone knows the old chestnut about how western civilization venerates thinness simply because our meals and bodies have become so super-sized and so, like moony-eyed teenagers with unrequited crushes, we all want what we can't have. Yet we seem to have entered a staring contest with thinness on this one, in that every year the definition of 'thin' becomes literally narrower and not – it has to be said – just by models but mainly by celebrities. Now that we are all so obsessed with thinness a person can become famous just for being thin – Nicole Richie springs nimbly if bonily to mind here – meaning that it's really celebrities who are getting thinner and models are having to keep up to stay within the public's increasingly warped perception of what is deemed to be slim. But to watch a hollow-eyed model with thighs thinner than her ankles, her arms pathetically covered with soft down in absence of any human fat to keep her warm, stumble mutely down a catwalk towards the aggressive mass of cameras is to see in action the phrase 'taking an idea too far'.

Newspapers get highly excited about the biannual Models Are Too Thin debate and how it affects women readers. It is an utterly reasonable, and probably long overdue, argument. But, truth be told, with the exception of a celebrity court case, or maybe a royal family gaff, nothing warms a news editor's heart more on a slow day than a story that can be illustrated with a photo of a pretty, thin woman. Funny, how the word 'hypocritical' seemed to float on the breeze there for a moment. Moreover, if some of the 'news'papers who have become particularly exercised on this subject were really so concerned about women's self-esteem perhaps they could consider giving certain other stories – such as how working women are damaging their children, that a bit of cellulite on a famous woman is cause for repulsion and how any woman over the age of thirty who isn't married and tied to a sink and mewling infant is selfish, stupid, probably celibate, or, alternatively, a sluttish tramp – a rest for, I don't know, a week maybe.

There is not so much a school as a mail-order course of thought that says the reason models have to be so skinny is because all designers are gay men and their idea of physical perfection is the body of a teenage boy and that's who they really want to, ahem, dress. We can swiftly dismiss this, and not just for its naked homophobia, and, yes, the word naked is being used advisedly. Briefly, any superstar designer with a million in the bank and a billion pairs of sunglasses to his name has, it's pretty fair to say, his pick of starstruck fashion student teenage boys to play with; he doesn't need to console himself with a bloodless, flat-chested teenage girl from Swindon. If a designer wanted to design for men, there is a little industry out there that he probably would have considered as a career alternative. It's called 'menswear'.

In fact, designers claim that models need to be thin so as not to interrupt their aesthetic, which is an impressively euphemistic way of saying that skinny people are easier to make clothes for as you don't have to worry about boring stuff like proper tailoring, flattering cuts or making space for bums and breasts. Instead you can have fun with exciting things like peacock feathers on dresses and oversized puffa jackets trimmed with chinchilla fur.

Thinness requisite aside, the concept of models is a little odd in general. The point of the model is to insinuate that if we buy that dress / perfume / designer iPod case we, too, will look as good as the model in the advertisement. Maybe this does work on some kind of subconscious level, but you have to wonder about the quality of an £800 handbag that itself needs to be accessorized with a £10,000-a-day supermodel in order to look hot. Wouldn't everyone be a lot more impressed with a shoe that made Christine Hamilton look like Christy Turlington instead of one that made Christy look like Christy?

Apparently not, because forty years on from Twiggy, centuries on from adoring portraits of society ladies and kings' mistresses, we all still love to look at photos of women prettier than us. And this is the real issue. Designers use models for one reason: not to give us all eating disorders, not just for the sheer hilarious hell of it, not because they actually think we should look like them, but to sell clothes. If we weren't persuaded by a photo of a skinny woman spritzing a bit of perfume on her clavicles, they would have ditched that technique years ago. Equally, to blame models for causing eating disorders, as though their thinness is a deliberate personal attack, is even more stupid than shooting the messenger, as the messenger is the designer – you're actually just shooting the messenger's blameless horse. The fashion industry doesn't actually give a fig what women look like – it's just interested in finding the body shape that hypnotizes customers into handing over their credit cards. So maybe we could all stop taking models as

personal affronts and see them for what they are – walking, talking advertisements, and feel, even, a twinge of pity while considering the physical exertions they suffer in the name of a probably not particularly fulfilling job.

To say that models cause anorexia is about as incisive as saying adverts for beer cause alcoholism. Eating disorders are not about wanting to be thin any more than being an alcoholic is about enjoying a pint with the boys: it is a mental illness and to coin a connection between vanity and anorexia is yet another example of the media belittling women (for it is, still, mainly women who suffer from anorexia although certainly recorded cases of male sufferers are rising) and making them sound like silly little children with too much time and too many copies of *Vogue* on their hands. Ooh, let's protect the childish little things from big bad scary Anna Wintour! Still, it's far easier to blame, say, Giorgio Armani for the rise of eating disorders than to ask why so many women in the twenty-first century still feel that the only way they can express any inner unhappiness is by harming themselves, I guess.

But this is not to let the fashion industry off the hook. Its veneration of hipbones validates the anorexic and bulimic's mindset because thinness is, incredibly, as highly valued as they think it is. It's like the old horror movie cliché: you wake up and it turns out that the nightmare actually is real and everyone does think the same as you. This may speed up a person's descent into the illness and it almost certainly will make it harder for them to recover from it – but it does not cause it.

Undoubtedly the fashion industry needs to expand its concept of what it considers female beauty. But fashion provides an exaggerated insight into what we view as beautiful. Only when that changes will there be models, and eventually celebrities, over seven and a half stone, older than twenty-two and maybe not almost always white, but let's not go too crazy here.

Money, *and when to spend it*

*T*hat fashion generally involves the expenditure of money is probably the most commonly cited criticism lobbed at it by its detractors. Quite when the western world came over all communist and decided that spending one's own money on oneself was a sign of unmitigated evil is not entirely clear. Nor is it fully explained why a bag with a four figure price tag is a sign of greater moral decrepitude than, say, the making of a terrible movie for $100 million (see *Vanity, the joys thereof*), or why a £700 dress that lasts for ever and makes you feel fabulous is less acceptable than a £700 holiday that is over in a fortnight, leaves carbon footprints all over the planet and is, if we're wholly honest, a bit of a pain in the arse.

Of course there is good fashion out there that doesn't cost half a month's salary, occasionally in the vintage market. But digging out a decent Chanel jacket from amongst a pile of moth-eaten kaftans and Granny tights requires time that most mortals simply do not have due to crazy things like work and Having A Life (see *Vintage*).

The all new and improved high street has confirmed that a lot of designer stuff is a knee-slappingly hilarious waste of money. A £40 jumper dress from the high street often looks remarkably similar to a £400 jumper dress from a designer. Designer pieces are usually (note that crucial hedging) better made than high street, but badly finished seams are why God invented dry cleaners. And sometimes, when you pick up another visibly poorly made designer blouse in Selfridges and then have a little chuckle at the price you do wonder if the designer just sits in his 'atelier' ('office' to the proles), knocks some piece of clothing out, chucks a little ball on his high-digit roulette table, giggles cocainishly when it lands on the £850 and then puts that on the price tag.

But none of this means you shouldn't occasionally buy something whose price makes your knees crumple in agony. People (i.e. your

mother) will sigh and say things like, 'Well, if you know you'll love it
and wear it for ever, then I guess . . .' but this is both unhelpful and
untrue. If people knew they were going to love something 'for ever'
then there would be no such thing as divorce lawyers. It probably
does make sense to spend money on something that you will wear
more than once but going by this logic it is better to spend £150 on
a designer T-shirt than £400 on a designer black tie gown unless
Barbara Cartland is your style guru and ballgowns are part of your
daily wardrobe. Certainly there are designer 'pieces' (again, another
touch of the parlance – see *Fashion speak*) that are superior to ones
you find on the high street, particularly shoes and bags.

But in truth, the only factor that should dictate whether or not
to buy something is how much you adore it right then. Yes, it really
is that simple.

Take away such distracting factors as articles in magazines telling you that this bag is 'essential this season', any photos you have
seen of Kate Moss carrying or wearing said item or just any brain-
fogging hangovers, boredom or break-up pain and ask yourself,
will the pleasure of owning this outweigh the guilt of paying for
it? Will you be actually excited when you wake up tomorrow and
see it in your wardrobe or will it be like the morning after a particularly misguided one night stand without the mitigating factor
of being able to get it out of your flat before breakfast? If the answers are yes, yes, no and if you can afford it without taking food
out of your children's mouths, risking the roof over your own fair
head, and you're not inadvertently funding some
hideous Chinese children's sweat shop
then, what the hell, just buy it. Life
is too short to spend it in bankruptcy, yes; but life is also too
short to spend it regretting that
amazing dress you didn't buy five
years ago that would have worked

perfectly with every date you've been on since, and every lady should give herself a present now and then.

People will often tell you that you shouldn't buy this season's It bag, dress or whatever a celebrity has recently been photographed wearing because (a) fashion victim status will duly be anointed on your personage (b) everyone else will have it, too, and (c) it will be So Over by next season. And all of these are just points, if a little unfair, as they assume the only thing that could make consumers desire something is if magazines and celebrities tell them that they should. If your adoration overpowers the knowledge that a lot of really annoying people will buy it as well, or that even more annoying people will sneer at it being 'last season' next season (although surely everything is, literally, last season when we reach next season, but pedantry is a most unattractive quality) and that you don't care, then what the devil.

You could consider some points, though. Ask among your trusted designer-buying friends which labels can be relied on for well-made clothes and accessories because some are definitely stronger in this department than others. Next, ask yourself honestly whether you will really be able to use or wear it more than three times. If the answer's no, head to the nearest coffee shop and do some solemn soul searching as to whether you want to own a £1,500 dress that you would ultimately have paid £500 for each time you wear it or will it cause nausea every time you open your wardrobe and, really, no woman should be put off her Weetabix every morning like that. And, finally, think of a friend or even celebrity whose taste you admire and (in a secular take on a Texan's favourite question, what would Jesus do?) ask yourself, what would they do (your friend or celebrity, not the Texan, mind)? This does not mean you should try to dress or look like someone else, but rather this person – at least in your mind – is less prone to making the kind of impetuous purchases that look so gorgeous on the shop floor only to transpire as something that the Hilton sisters would have rejected for being a bit *de trop*.

Life can be pretty boring sometimes, and a little depressing, too. So ultimately everyone could stop beating themselves up quite so harshly at the idea of spending money on clothes and the world really would continue to spin. You're not eating small children, you're not flogging arms, you're just buying a damn dress.

This is not to say you should come over all Ivana Trump and forget that designer fodder should be considered a treat, not the taken-for-granted norm. After all, like Marmite or other substances with which some designers and models are more *au fait* than yeast-based spreads, designer pieces are only good when used sparingly. If fashion is about self-indulgence, the occasional guilt-free expenditure denotes someone who knows they are worthy of the occasional sporadic spoil and they don't need anyone else to do this for them; head to toe ab-fabness says you only accrue self-esteem from having a screechingly camp dead designer's name on a tag at the back of your skirt.

Moss, Kate, *and how she ruined your wardrobe*

*T*here are many mind-teasing questions about Kate Moss. Does she really think singing is a good career move? How did no one notice that her name should be cockney slang for weight loss until Lily Allen pointed it out? And how on earth could she have gone from Johnny Depp – Johnny Depp, for God's sake! – to that incoherent and incapacitated Pete Doherty?

The most interesting one of all, though, is regarding her role in life. To whit, this young lady has not started a single fashion trend that has benefitted womankind. Admittedly, this is not generally cause for excommunication from the human species but is a bit of a sticking point for someone who is frequently described as a 'trend setter'.

Pirate boots, hot pants, waistcoats, pixie haircuts, expensive vintage dresses, fur, skinny jeans, high-waisted jeans – all started by Mossy, all harbingers of more aesthetic harm to the female populace than hair crimpers.

So perhaps the real question here is not so much about Moss but rather – solemn dip of the head – about us. Because although most women have learned painful lessons from some if not all of the above, we persist in studiously following Moss's every wardrobe decision, certain that she has found some heretofore unknown fashion trick or garment that will turn us all into, well, her. The fact is that after several thousand years of getting dressed there is very little in the way of clothing that remains unplumbed, hence the constant recycling of trends (see *Decade rehashing and why designers live in the past*). What Moss does is find something that would look terrible on most people but looks quite good on her. Gather close, children, because here is an important lesson: that is why she is a model and you are not (see *Models*).

So while it is understandable that designers love her, it is less clear why so many women do, too, considering the damage she has wreaked in their wardrobes, bank accounts and general dignity.

Yet one could see this as rather cheering proof of women's self-love and eternal sunniness. Contrary to all the guff about models destroying women's self-confidence, the fact that so many bought nasty suede boots with weird buckles in the belief that this would make them look like an underweight photogenic twenty-something really does suggest a commendable level of optimism and faith in one's natural appearance. And Kate, God bless her, keeps on proving this again and again as each trend she starts becomes increasingly unflattering to women, yet still they follow in her pixie-booted footprints. It's a stonkingly clever strategy on her part to disprove all the media's whinging about Moss being a bad example and the single-handed cause for eating disorders because anorexia, you know, never existed until 1991. Bless you, Kate. Bless you and your high-waisted jeans.

Party dresses, *and what yours says about you*

*W*hen it comes to party dresses there is only one command-
ment: wear an outfit that makes you feel good. This, however, often gets confused with a distantly related, but very, very different rule: dress in what you think is desired by the opposite sex.
This tends to result in an aesthetically distressing gap yawning open
between wishful thinking and impressive self-delusion. Hence the
all too common sight of a winsomely girlish party dress on a woman
most definitely old enough to know better and therefore making
herself look not so much like Cinderella at the ball as her batty fairy
godmother (the reader is referred to images of Barbara Cartland, God
rest her pink taffeta soul, for further illustration). Conversely, while
it is all well and good to use a party to reveal your heretofore hidden
wild sexual depths, the sight of a shy woman gritting her teeth determinedly in a lycra leopard-print dress and sashaying desperately
in front of her long secretly desired quarry probably wouldn't even
have served as a turn on to Warren Beatty, the pre-OAP years.

The real difficulty with finding a good party dress is that, with
this outfit more than any other, most women aspire to please
simultaneously three very different groups, all with widely diverg-
ing expectations and requisites: the opposite sex, your friends and
you. Kate Moss, unsurprisingly, is the master of how to do this with
her penchant for shimmery (fun for her), long (respect from her girl
friends for going down such a maverick party dress route) and body
clinging (hello, boys) party gowns. But then, she has had a fair bit of
practice so don't feel too much of a comparative failure.

On top of the practical difficulties no other outfit is more
revealing about the wearer than the party garb. On the flip side of
youthful delusions and dubious aspirations of femme fatale status
is what has been referred to as the lamb dressed as mutton: a young
women who embraces with unseemly enthusiasm and premature

haste middle-aged styles of dressing. Sometimes this is because they are Sloanes and therefore we need not worry about them too much because wearing silk neck scarves and cable-knit jumpers seems to make them happy, seeing as they have been doing it for almost thirty years. For women outside of the SW3 and 6 postcodes, it is often out of shyness. Dressing like a middle-aged frump helps to head off expectations that they might be the life of the party and they can scuttle off back home a.s.a.p. It's the sartorial equivalent of that wretchedly common female tendency, self-deprecation. This is not just a shame but a self-made vicious circle because if there's anything that will put the dampener on any potential inner sparkle it's wearing some mumsy blouse, badly fitted jeans and scruffy flats. Here is a party outfit that positively screams crippling inner repression. And as we've already said about repressed feelings, they then come bursting out in one inappropriately large gush, hence the leopard-print lycra which can but only send the poor woman rushing back for the cover of her beige blouse. Ladies, ladies, there is a middle path! Even just a simple LBD with perhaps a bit of detailing around the neck, or a bit of a style twist, such as a bared one shoulder or a gentle pouf to the skirt or, if you're feeling particularly wild, a spot of beading will put you in a much better mood and not make you feel like you're the after-dinner entertainment on a package holiday to Marbella.

There are lots of 'fun' party dresses out there, with their ruffles (see *Ruffles, from French ingénue to Bozo the clown*), patterns (see *Patterns – or test patterns?*) and velvet detailing (see *Velvet, and why it should be banned*). But as that ominous slew of parentheses suggests, these are fraught – fraught, I tell thee – with great danger to the wearer. Namely, that while each can work when treated with caution, too often designers throw this, along with taste, practicalities and general decency, to the wind when it comes to the party dress. Moreover, it's difficult to believe that the women themselves are having much fun in these overly embellished confections: rather, they have been collectively brainwashed by magazines trying to appease their advertisers and retailers desperately trying to shift their stock that the amount of intrusive detailing on a dress is in direct proportion to the excitement the dress will provide and its value for money.

Worse is the mistranslation so many men and women make in regards to the word 'fun' in the fashion context. A 'fun' dress should mean something that makes you look and feel witty and dazzling, not like you work part-time as Chintzy the Clown. Of course, you don't want to just wear some boring black cocktail dress as if you were Barbara Amiel swanning about at some tedious high-powered do with Henry Kissinger. But a compromise can be found between some nondescript tasteful shift and a bright pink satin affair decked with bows and sequins that even Vanessa Feltz might deem a bit much.

It cannot be stressed too often – although heaven knows this book will try (see *Heels, the highs, the lows and when fat is better than thin*) – how completely and utterly stupid it is to wear painful shoes to a party. Even if you're wearing the most amazing dress in the history of the universe – verily, one that has been dipped in a magic potion guaranteed to make all who see you prostrate themselves at your feet in awe of your fabulousness – if your shoes are painful your dress will be for naught as you will spend the evening feeling miserable, grumpy and boring. So dresses that can be worn with pretty flats are invaluable and all the heelophiles out there will be surprised at how many of them there are out there. With the exception of just below the knee and mid-calf, flats can be worn with just about any length of dress. Although your legs may look less 'toned' than they do in heels this is not necessarily a bad thing, seeing as in this instance 'toned' is a euphemism for 'throbbing with pain'. And anyway, for all the knee-jerk sneers we make about men's shallow depths, the truth is that the worthy ones would far rather spend an evening with a lady whose legs might not be hoiked up to her armpits, but is able to carry on a witty conversation as opposed to a long-limbed goddess who spends the night sitting grouchily in the corner with a facial expression that suggests she needs to switch to All-Bran.

Chunky-heeled boots are also useful in this regard if the thought of wearing flats at a party makes you inwardly, if misguidedly, recoil. These are great with tunic dresses, which have been one of the best recent boons to women in regards to party dresses. Essentially long T-shirts, these allow a lady – of any age, incidentally – to eat without annoying waistband strangulation, dance because they are amenably loose and look good in a way that appeals to her friends, potential onlookers and herself. They are loose, short, cool and modest, four highly desirably party-dress qualities, three of which are in all too short commodity.

A similar point can be made about keeping warm. Again, it is an all too common assumption made by partygoing ladies that the more flesh they show the sexier they are. This may well be the case in the eyes of some young men, but do you really want to leave with an aspiring swain who chooses his women by how much of their shoulders is on display? Again, it is far more attractive to see a woman in, say, a long-sleeved short dress and tights (an outfit that looks brilliant with, yes, flats) laughing and chatting and dancing all night than one in a spaghetti-strapped slip shivering miserably by the radiator and incapable of even saying 'yes' when asked if she'd like to dance as her lips have frozen together.

Other than the inadvisability of Cartlandesque pink, there are no rules in regard to colours and lengths of party dresses. It's all about what makes you feel at your most dazzling. For this reason, metallics are quite useful in providing the always welcome shimmer factor (thus quoth R.E.M: people who are shiny are people who are happy) without recourse to sequins, which will often make you look like you're wearing an eight year old's art project. But make sure your metallics are slightly dulled to head off any BacoFoil jokes. The one exception to the anti-sequin rule is if the sequins are the same colour as the fabric as they then can look surprisingly tasteful, particularly in black. They will, however, still fall off the dress, as sequins almost always do, meaning that, like Hansel and Gretel, you will leave a little trail behind you all evening, which might be quite useful should your friends lose you but is a right devil to clean up when you're running around your flat beforehand getting ready. Of course, black is the most useful just in terms of being able to wheel the old girl out the most often (and that refers to the dress, by the way, not you) without obnoxious people passing sarky comment (and if they do a brief reply is advised, one that involves the words 'life', 'get' and 'a' in appropriate order.) Instead, party dresses are one of those rare purchases for which you don't – shouldn't, even – need to make a token effort of remembering whether mustard, pleats, dropped waist or whatever is in this season: even fashion people know that this is one scenario in which looking good trumps looking trendy, hence Moss's long-term devotion to one style.

You should also have some fun (and that word is being used with caution) with your party dress, if only to maintain your perkiness should the party itself begin to flag. This might mean wearing a heretofore untried style or what American TV psychotherapists call 'stepping out of your comfort zone'. Of course, you shouldn't step so far out that you become a socially crippled stranger in a strange land (*pace*, the shy girl in the leopard-print dress). But if you're generally a loose, let it all hang out, kinda lady, at least try on a structured cocktail dress when you're on the shopping hunt, or if you're a floor-length gal, give a mini-tunic dress a go. Neither of these are particularly difficult styles and a party is probably the one place you can try out a new look without being on the receiving end of too many annoying comments simply because everyone goes for a bit of self-reinvention at a party. Plus, it just makes sense to have some variety in your wardrobe instead of repeatedly, if subconsciously, merely buying basically the same dress over and over and over.

Sometimes it's nice to pretend you're someone else for the evening (in a non-mentally unhinged way), or just to take yourself out of your usual worries and neuroses for a night, and it's ultimately cheaper and definitely more attractive to do this through a dress as opposed to the alternative approach by partygoers, drugs.

This is why it is not all that ridiculous (which doesn't mean that it isn't a little ridiculous) that so many women insist on buying a new dress for every party: if a party provides the opportunity for fantasy self-reinvention, then wearing a dress speckled with snake-bite stains from the time you dribbled down your top during a drinking competition at your best friend's thirtieth really isn't going to help you escape the memories of your sordid past.

Office parties are a whole other bag of chips. The problem with the office 'do', as it is all too often referred to, leading to the inevitable wag in the building referring to it as the office 'don't', is that your goal with your outfit here is so different from that of your normal garden-variety party – namely, to impress your mates and to make every man in the room wish, to quote the wisdom of Kylie, that they could be so lucky. Of course, this latter goal may well, in fact, be your intention at the office party due to a long-nurtured, hands-brushing-over-the-photocopier crush, but the reader is strongly counselled against pursuing this, mainly because it can only end in one of two ways. Either, a nasty break-up resulting in crippling awkwardness every time the two of you come into work, a custody fight over the canteen and having to make an effort to look good every sodding morning so that he can see what he's missing. Or two, marriage, which doesn't necessarily preclude the aforementioned eventuality anyway.

So leaving that aside, the goal of an office party is to look nice, perhaps a little more interesting than the generic high-street wrap dresses every other woman will be wearing, if only to show colleagues that you are far superior to them, but nothing too interesting that will attract sarky comments all night from John in Accounts or, more annoyingly, your boss. More pressingly, while you want to look nice you would probably like to get through the evening without any drunken propositions, gropes or anyone's eyeballs looking like they're about to embark on a scuba-diving venture into your cleavage. So think a nice plain dress, knee length ideally, black almost certainly, but perhaps with a slash neck, bell sleeves or maybe some detailing along the hem – something, anyway, to show a bit of au courant style awareness (all bosses like to see that their employees are down wit' da yoof and only in an office party is this somehow proven via some bell sleeves from Reiss). A trouser suit can also work as long as you leave early before John gets too drunk and starts making lesbian jokes. And then inwardly repeat the following mantra all night: 'friendly but aloof, friendly but aloof'.

For weddings, there is no choice but to dress in something anonymously generic and just suck it down. A wedding is the bride's day and any guest who turns up in some amazing Roland Mouret cocktail dress or whatever limited edition Balenciaga slip that Kristen Scott Thomas was recently photographed wearing is not only being selfish but stupid. Weddings are one of three occasions from which the photos are guaranteed to last for ever (the other two being births and really bad holidays). And as anyone who has ever seen photos from a 1970s wedding knows, nothing looks more comical to future generations than overly fashionable party clothes from times gone by. This doesn't mean you have to embrace the wedding guest cliché too enthusiastically; in fact, even though you're going to have to take one day off from your lifetime mission of pushing fashion forward you could focus your energy today on showing the world that going to a wedding needn't result in the Pavlov's-dog instinctive reaction of reaching for the floral bias-cut skirt from Paul Smith, a pastel top from Jigsaw and an Hermès silk scarf. Instead, something from the shift-dress family, a sleeveless fitted top with a modest plain skirt or well-cut light-coloured trousers with a smart blouse and a hat that doesn't make you look like Kew Gardens on legs would work just grand, ensuring that you will probably look the best in the photos, but in such a subtle way that no one can accuse you of trying to steal the bride's limelight. Ha ha.

Party shirts, *the fun lovin' guy's staple*

*G*od bless the man in the party shirt! Here is a heterosexual (and the party shirt sporter is *always* heterosexual) male who truly respects the power of fashion. In fact, a lot of straight men are in far more awe of fashion power than women, as proven by the fact that quite a number of them seem to think that sporting a pink shirt might be sufficient to alter their sexual orientation, or at least make people think they have (see *Masculinity, and the clothes that challenge it*) whereas women, judging by the annual return of 'masculine tailoring', don't seem to harbour such qualms.

Et voilà, the party shirt, the favoured weapon of a man who is probably not known for his wild and crazy ways, but, oh, how he wishes he were. And so, party-shirt man, or PSM, believes that if he just slips on a certain button-down shirt by Paul Smith, not so much patterned but veritably mosaiced with some kind of hideous design, he will undergo a Superman-like transformation and his party-animal nature will be revealed to all.

This in itself is rather sweet, but the real kicker is how PSM only owns one of these shirts. That is how much faith he has in the shirt's effect: its powers will not diminish by overuse. Thus, the very same shirt comes out for every party, its fit perhaps altering slightly over the years, one more button coming undone with each passing office Christmas party, but its Rorschach-like pattern never, incredibly, fading. It is the most remarkable reversal of most females' mentality in that they believe one must never wear the same dress to multiple parties as people will notice and cast you out in disgust. Yet PSM is too wise for such nonsense as he knows that the effects of the shirt compensate for the sneers.

Patterns – *or test patterns?*

*L*ike curly hair and body weights of over nine stone, patterned clothes have been a victim of – deep breath, sonorous tone of voice – the Celebrity Culture in Which We Live. Oscar, schmoscar, due to the increasingly prevalent belief that a person's career can be destroyed by the quick snap of a paparazzi camera and the heartless placement of the photo in the Fashion

Disaster!!! section of a magazine, the most important achievement a celebrity can notch up is an ability to pick out clothes that will photograph well. This is why, for all the extra publicity they might bring, celebrities are ultimately very frustrating for a designer. With the occasional and salute-worthy exception of the likes of Sofia Coppola and – snore – Kate Moss, most celebrities aren't interested in looking fashionable; they're interested in looking good, and as anyone who has ever read an article in a fashion magazine proclaiming the fashionability of, say, smock dresses, empire lines or high-waisted trousers knows, these are two very different propositions. Being fashionable is ostensibly about wearing a look that is different from what has long been the mainstream norm and this determined, occasionally even blinkered, pursuit of novelty does not always photograph well, as all of the above examples have proven in their time. Some might argue that it's good for designers to have their more outré tendencies forcibly reined in by dint of having to placate the celebrities. Yet it is a little pitiful to see a man who wiled away his boyhood dreaming about the indelible impact he would make on the fashion world and then spent his mother's life savings going to fashion college now spending his adult life making party dresses that will look good on *In Style*'s red carpet round-up pages.

One thing that rarely looks good on those elite pages is a pattern. Patterns aren't slimming, there's no argument with that one; they don't make tend to make you look younger; they rarely even make you look taller: strike three! Yerrrrr outta there!

This is a real darn shame because a patterned garment can be a glorious thing. For a start, it's just dull wearing block colours day in, day out, no matter how flattering they might be on your complexion. Yet because celebrities are now so influential on designers and often on the way we dress, patterns have been sadly pushed to the back of the fashion queue.

Of course, some patterns are far superior to others: fey, mimsy, whimsical floral patterns have been beaten into ignominy due to overuse at Sloaney weddings; polka dots, which we have already discussed in this book and will probably do so again at some point, are problematic in their evocation of Minnie Mouse and their association with women who think that looking as childlike as possible is a bit of a winner as opposed to being just plain disturbing; horizontal stripes will make you resemble the Stay Puft Marshmallow Man who terrorized the city of New York at the end of *Ghostbusters*, and look how he ended up. Paisley makes you look like a walking lava lamp. There is no question that tartan is what is referred to in fashion speak as 'tricky' (i.e. pretty bloody hideous) and will generally make you look like you're moonlighting for the Scottish Tourist Board. But when done in relatively subtle and similar colours, such as extra pale blues, greens and yellows as opposed to the traditional scarlet affair it can be surprisingly bearable. Just don't wear it on a button-down shirt with a pair of jeans unless you're going for a *Deliverance* kinda look today. Celia Birtwell's gorgeous line drawings are one of the rare patterns – indeed, possibly the only pattern – that look as lovely on a person as they would hanging up on a wall. Liberty prints have a kitsch appeal so can only be worn in measured doses unless you want to be mistaken for being part of the set from a carefully preserved 1930s house. Marc by Marc Jacobs is fantastic for vaguely retro seventies patterns which are nowhere near as hideous as that description would suggest: think instead of bold mini-floral patterns, star prints and other similar styles worn by the kids on Sesame Street back in its early years.

Tellingly, the other womenswear labels that do patterns particularly well – Marni and Miu Miu – are very much labels that girls get and boys often don't (see *Get, fashion that girls do and boys don't*). While a patterned top is by no means as boy-offensive as an egg-shaped dress, it's not ideal simply because it intrudes on the man's purpose. For men, a woman's clothes are there to make the woman herself look better when they are gazing at her. Patterns therefore make for an unnecessary distraction. For a woman, seeing as she's sporting the clothes all day, she often wants to wear something that can maintain her interest for a couple of hours, hence the appeal of something with a little more to look at than a plain white blouse. It's a bit like wearable TV without the risk of accidentally finding yourself face to face with Anthea Turner.

This isn't exactly the most insurmountable hurdle you'll come across in your life: for a start, you don't always need to dress for men. But you can also compromise, which, frankly, isn't such a bad idea when it comes to patterns. The first hard and fast and rather obvious rule is, only one patterned garment at a time. This is why it is never advisable to buy a patterned coat. For a start, even the most pattern-happy female might weary of wearing the same pattern every day. Next, one has to be in a certain mood – generally a good one – in order to carry off a pattern. Having to wear a polka-dot winter coat when you're hungover, recently dumped, on the verge of being sacked and generally a bit naffed off with the world is really not going to help your general outlook. (See *Coats, stuck at the nexus point between dull and stressful.*)

Next, think about where you're wearing the pattern. Patterns may serve as a distraction from your pretty face, but they definitely do not distract from your body. So if you'd rather people didn't stare at your hips and upper thighs, which suddenly seem to be looking two and a half times their normal size, don't wear patterns on the lower half of your body.

But the real disadvantage to patterns is their noticibility factor. Patterned clothes jump up and down in front of onlookers faces shrieking, 'Look at me! Look at me!'; plain ones are the shy, slightly mousey siblings who stand quietly in the corner. And while we could all do with stepping out of the corner now and again, there is something to be said for tasteful subtlety.

So you really love your new Marc by Marc jumper with the kitschy heart pattern, don't you? Well, by the end of the week everyone else will know how much you love it, too, because it's a little harder getting away with wearing a particular patterned itemed more than two days in a row than it is with a plain one, not unless you want to be known as 'that woman who is always wearing that heart print jumper'. Thus you not only have to do the wash more often (nightmare), but you have to keep some kind of mental timetable charting down when you last wore that heart jumper, and that splodge-print top, and that beaded cardigan, and that Celia Birtwell for Topshop dress, guaranteeing that you're leaving a respectable amount of time between each outing so that the neighbours don't begin to talk. And really, is that why God gave you a brain?

Pink

Women – kind of annoying, aren't they? All that sobbing into their Chardonnay about men, counting the calories of a carrot juice and singing along to Chaka Khan with only a hairbrush and a mirror for special effects – pshaw! Oh, sorry, the spirit of a TV sitcom 'writer' seems to have hijacked this book. After all, it's not like any of us really do any of the above. Well, not in front of a TV camera. Anyway, one female stereotype that I will grant does seem to have some truth is a general fondness for pink. Obviously, this is all the fault of the parents with that pink for girls, blue for boys nonsense. But, really, you'd think a thirty-year-old woman would have been able to progress beyond trying to recapture the colour of her first babygro. Until men reclaim this colour for their own – and, frankly, it's ridiculous that they don't, seeing as the shade often suits their stubbly complexions far better than it suits a woman's peachy one – it will continue to be used and abused as the tonal code for girlish femininity.

Pink accessories are cause for particular concern. 'Don't fear!' they cry. 'I may have money to buy my own handbags but, really, I'm just a sweet, unthreatening girl at heart, who wishes she could still play with her Apple Blossom My Little Pony!' For this reason, they are almost more grating than a head-to-toe pink outfit – yes, even a (shudder) pink velour tracksuit – which might suggest a certain Glinda from *The Wizard of Oz* hang-up, but at least is so ridiculous that it can be swiftly dismissed. Relegating the pink to the accessories is somehow worse because now there is not even the illusion of irony; just the pretence of subtlety, coupled with a decided lack of shame. The difference between a long pink party dress and a pair of babyish pink shoes peeking out from beneath a pair of black trousers is like the difference between a fully paid-up Creationist and someone who appears utterly normal until they let slip some reference to how dinosaur bones are just an archaeologist's 'conspiracy'. Show me a woman in a pair of pink kitten heels and decked with a pink beaded shawl, and I'll show you a lady with James Blunt on secret repeat.

Plastic surgery *and how all those 1950s horror B-movies weren't so far off the mark*

S o it turns out the zombies really are taking over the planet: huge swathes of the population actually have been brainwashed into flinging themselves on to the tables of possibly dodgy doctors in order to become members of some homogenous, dehumanized tribe, and they have started to speak in strange, once-unimaginable tongues with phrases such as 'knee lifts' and 'hand Botox' becoming part of everyday parlance in women's magazines and certain planetary areas.

That England has succumbed to the madness has been to some, perhaps naively, a bit of a surprise. As with beauty spas and nail bars (see *Manicures, pedicures and the ever-rising bar of personal upkeep*), sure, we once thought, the (sarcastic moue) Americans might get into this, them with their super-sized quadruple-decker cheese burgers, psychotic exercise regimes and general bovine stupidity, snicker snicker. Trust them to try to take the short cut to physical perfection all the while scoffing down a two-kilo bag of some kind of rehydrated potato snack, so orange it could well be the original source of polonium 210. And, yeah, sure, the (patronizing sneer) Spanish and Italians would go for it, with their shamelessly brassy pursuit of the body beautiful. And maybe even the (knowing dip of the head to show awareness but never disapproval of cultural differences) Japanese would board this bandwagon, seeing as they've been going for whitening creams and so on for years. But never the English: oh, no, not the no-nonsense, proudly scruffy, stoutly batty English with their threadbare carpet bags and sensible footwear. But then, spit spot, Botox bars are scattered throughout the British capital like pubs, with the rest of the country following suit. Between 2005 and 2006, the number of people who had plastic surgery increased by a third; Botox, meanwhile, went up by more than 50 per cent.

Even the *Mail on Sunday* – the *Mail on flipping Sunday* – has a plastic surgery column offering advice on how to 'nip and tuck'. Leaving aside the matter of whether you would actually turn to a publication that still finds photos of oddly shaped root vegetables worthy of a double page spread over a decade after even Esther Rantzen stopped finding them funny for advice about how best to knife up your body, this really is a most extraordinary state of affairs. This newspaper rather fancies itself as the bastion of the traditional, the buffer against the tide of shallow modernity and the protector of all-gathered-round-the-hearth family values. Yet here it is, advising women how best to proceed in this most modern and shallow self-obsession. Admittedly, it does fit in with this publication's fixation with the female body and all its flaws, but one might have thought that plastic surgery's association with American wackiness would rule it out of relevancy to the *Wail on Sunday*. One would have been wrong.

There were warning signs of the encroaching tide of Botox that has tsunamied the country. Just as these homogenous American coffee bars make every street in Britain – in the world now, actually – look pretty much the same and offer nothing but fake coffee (Christmas-themed coffee – I mean, honestly), so these surgical procedures make everyone look the same and create nothing but fake humans. For proof, just look at a picture of Joan Rivers: is your reaction (a) 'My gosh, look at that sexy, lithe young teenager!' or (b) 'Good God, the aliens have landed!' And despite Rivers openly admitting that this is due to plastic surgery as opposed to proximity to a nuclear power plant with a rather dodgy safety record, this has proven to be no dissuasion to the ever-increasing masses signing up for a little bit of what she's having.

I am all for a woman doing something that makes her feel better about herself: if that bump on her nose has made her so self-conscious that she avoids turning to the left in public then, by all means, if she has the money and knows a good doctor, why shouldn't she get it ironed out? (Because it will be bloody painful and there's no guarantee that it will really work yet, hey, a lady can but try.) And I have no truck with the theory that it is somehow 'anti-feminist' to have plastic surgery because it encourages a false perception in how a woman should look: honey, if your views of how a normal woman looks are so fragile that they can be dismantled by a glance at some plastic, airbrushed woman then you are not smart enough to call yourself a feminist. Plus, it's a pointless argument: if words like 'scalpels', 'bloodied bone shavings' and 'six weeks of looking like a victim of domestic abuse' don't dissuade the potential surgical customer, it seems unlikely that 'not doin' it for the sisters' will.

The real problem with this astonishing escalation in plastic surgery is that the industry has, rather cleverly, found more and more procedures a person can have, giving them complexes about parts of the body heretofore rarely considered. No longer are we in the age of a simple nip and tuck or lipo. Now every last crevice needs attending to. Hand Botox quickly comes to mind. Cheek implants follow.

And let us not forget ear touch-ups, of course, for those troublesome creases in your lobe. It is the rare plastic surgery clinic that will not mention these to you and more.

And why shouldn't they? They need your money, of course they're going to try to sell you more. It's like feigning shock that kids' sugary food companies dare to buy advertising time during children's TV shows: when else are they going to try to flog their oversweetened fruit juices or their breakfast cereals that are little more than sugar cubes in milk – during a midnight porn show? (Actually, that might work quite well, seeing as that demographic probably represents the rest of their customer base.) This is called capitalism, my friends, in which everyone is out to make money. The only question is how the public responds to the solicitations and the real surprise is just how quickly the public rose to the plastic surgery industry's decidedly unenticing bait. If anyone wanted to make an argument that women are just simple little children, so easily led and in need of sheltering censorship, then this is it. Forget about the fuss over skinny models, the rise in plastic surgery is the absolute corker when it comes to proof.

True devotees of the form have come up with a rather ingenious explanation/excuse for their recreational pursuit: they call it 'taking care or looking after oneself'. Like I said, ingenious, not just for the suggestion that fighting against nature's given course is on a par with going on a yoga retreat, but also for the idea that injecting oneself with general anaesthetics and neurotoxin botulinum toxin A, as Botox is properly if not very temptingly known, is somehow tantamount to giving up sugar in its health-giving qualities. Trudie-she's-married-to-Sting-y'know-Tyler has become the poster girl for this dichotomy, apparently seeing no contradiction between her insistence on only eating organic food that has been fed on the tears of virgin angels and her regular appointments with her Botox doctor. But then, maybe the botulinum is organic too – who are we to sneer?

This is known as the Driving the Car to the Gym kind of mentality in its self-hypocrisy. Quite why a person would spend three and half times more on organic food in order to duck all those scary carcinogenic pesticides, only then to proffer up their faces once a month to be injected straight into their foreheads with a toxin that was once considered a potential chemical weapon is just one of those funny mysteries life occasionally lobs our way. Well, at least their corpses will be marvellously wrinkle free.

Ladies, is this really what you spent all those years earning money for, studying for, working for: preventing your hands from ageing? Swapping Botox doctor numbers? Having needles stuck in your extremities in order to look (ooh, sexy!) permanently startled and facially stapled? And, moreover, why should we continue the already too prevalent trend of women suffering such physical discomfort in the name of aesthetic so-called perfection while men occasionally saunter to the gym but in all other respects become the fat and hairy pigs nature intended for us all in middle and older age? If there's one thing to embrace about growing older it is that one hopefully achieves enough inner wisdom to relinquish all the self-loathing and self-obsession that is the tax one pays for being young. The only other alternative is to spend your life hating your natural body, railing against the unalterable rhythms of nature and paying ever increasing amounts of money and pain in a vain (in all senses of the word) attempt to fight it.

So perhaps it makes sense that the *Mail on Sunday* has become so at ease with the concept of plastic surgery, seeing as a photo of Madonna's forty-something hands seem to cause its sister publication, the *Daily Mail*, such distress every few months.

For the rest of us, is this really how you want to spend your life, easing the pain of the *Daily Mail*'s picture editor?

Prada, *the frumpy but fashionable*

*P*rada styles itself as the label it's OK for intellectual feminists to like. You have to wonder how precarious these women's self-image must be if they think it might somehow be damaged by showing an interest in fashion, and it is on this kind of knife-edge, poised between careful cerebralism and artificial poseur, that Prada balances.

Prada's reputation as the acceptably intellectual label stems primarily from the designer, Miuccia Prada. Rare is the profile of Mrs Prada, as she is known, despite Prada actually being her maiden name, that does not make reference to her university degree and youthful dalliance with communism, as if they were proof of her unique cerebralism. In regard to the former, this carries the not really very accurate suggestion that everyone else in fashion is an uneducated cave dweller who probably thinks Chekhov is a pattern one should be sporting this season. In regard to the latter, some might question whether a move from communism to fashion designer is more suggestive of a remarkable fluidity of personal values than a show of deep intellect, but that belief seems to be in the minority judging from the tones of awe in which this biographical fact is constantly repeated.

Particularly interesting is how this label has retained its tight grip on this image of high intellect despite being just as if not more celebrity – and logomania – dependent than any other Italian labels, such as Gucci and Versace.

For a start, its fashion line came to mass fashion prominence when Uma Thurman wore a lilac Prada dress to the Oscars in 1999 and looked, as Uma tends to do, quite nice. Next, the advertisement campaigns for its sister label Miu Miu almost invariably star a celebrity, such as Selma Blair or Lindsay Lohan, neither noted for the height of their brows. And, finally, the whole Prada bag mania only started because Miuccia rather cleverly put the brand's label on the outside of those rather nasty little knapsacks the company knocked out in the late eighties, thus making an item that looked like it should cost about £15 from Snow & Rock into a full-on snob-value fashion accessory. You have to wonder how all that fits in with the ol' communist credo.

Ultimately, though, it's the clothes that give Prada its image of quirky intellectualism. Turbans, big fluffy neon-coloured coats last seen on Carnaby Street in the sixties, frumpy and slightly wonky tweed skirts, William Morris print dresses, knitted leggings – all these have featured on Prada's catwalks in recent years. You will occasionally see a simple pretty dress or sexy jewelled top, but mainly Prada is a label that places oddness over conventional sex appeal. Although you might quibble whether a woman has to dress like a sociology lecturer, circa 1977, in order to feel that she is dressing for herself as opposed to society's expectations, there is always something to be said for a label more interested in the woman wearing the clothes than the man looking at them. That Mrs Prada does this and is then lauded by her colleagues as being the great intellect in the midst as opposed to a barking, hairy seventies throwback is proof that maybe the fashion industry isn't quite the chauvinist beast it is often accused of being.

Red carpet, *and what we can learn from it*

*N*ot much, and certainly not much compared to the coverage it gets in every form of national press these days, from po-faced broadsheets to screeching weekly celeb mags. Aside from providing yet another excuse for the press to publish lots of photos of half-undressed attractive and famous people, the appeal of the red carpet is easy to grasp.

Contrary to what magazines and, more commonly, celebrity

stylists with their eyes on their jobs make out, what a celebrity wears to a big event is not all that important. Yeah, sure, it will get them coverage in the papers the next day, but, ultimately, compared to the movie or album they make, it's fairly irrelevant. Björk is still trilling away despite the swan debacle and Meryl Streep is still some-how lauded as a fairly respectable actress despite her astonishing oversight in never wearing anything particularly memorable to an awards ceremony. And they dared to give her an Oscar or two; I mean, I ask you.

Instead, the real appeal comes from the insinuation that, here, we're getting a glimpse of the celeb off-duty; that it's an insight into their real personality, even if that insight begins and ends at whether they are a full- or knee-length kinda lady. In truth, of course, now that the red carpet gets so much attention and is seen as such a career maker and breaker any possible insight into a spontaneous show of genuine personality has been destroyed as swiftly as Björk's swan dress probably was back in 2001.

Many people are hugely grateful to the red carpet – mainly celeb-rity stylists and those luckless fashion assistants on magazines whose job it is to compile those always insightful 'trends from the red car-pet' picture spreads, it being so useful to know that three women wore blue to the I'm Brilliant, Me, Awards last month. It is now not so much an open secret as just plain open how much preparation goes into dressing for the red carpet and how little of it has to do with the celebrities themselves. Worse, with images of Björk's swan and Celine Dion's home-made backwards tuxedo dancing through their minds, most celebrities understandably if disappointingly err on the side of blandness. So if anything can be learned from the red carpet it is this: when in doubt, go for the beige, both in terms of dress colours and movie choices (ref. Jennifer Aniston).

Another difficulty is that the aim of a celebrity on a red carpet – to catch the eyes of as many paparazzi as possible – should not be that of most people on a daily basis. Thus, men should not wear monochrome outfits – white shirts with white jackets, ditto for black – unless they want to look like, respectively, ice-cream van vendors or hired assassins. Even worse are – ho ho – inverted tuxedos. You know, the black shirt with white bow tie (see *Classics with a twist*) combo – very nineties, you know. For women, red carpet dressing is just impractical seeing as it generally involves full-length gowns (a right bugger on anything other than, indeed, a red carpet) and plunging fronts and you are not allowed to carry accessories of any kind (proof, yet again, that celebrities occupy a different planetary dimension than the rest of us. Do they not have to lock their front doors in Hollywood? Where are their damn house keys?) But there are lessons to be gleaned. For one, if you decide to wear a backless dress you must apparently accept that, in exchange for all the attention you will receive you have to spend the evening standing backwards to everyone to show off your exciting bare back, turning your face around to make a minxy moue (ref. Renée Zellwegger). It's an odd concept, this dress style, because although its sexiness factor seems to lie in its proof that you are not wearing a bra, surely this then means that you must be very flat-chested, and while there is nothing wrong with that, it does suggest that certain elements of the fashion industry's aesthetic preferences have now well and truly infected the celebrity world and beyond. If you decide to go for the high slit style, you will apparently be overwhelmed with the desire to spend the evening leaning back on one leg and sticking your other leg through it to emphasize your daring style choice (ref. Liz Hurley). Again, not generally a winner in the practicality stakes or, in fact, anywhere off a red carpet unless you fancy spending an evening debating with a police officer about what constitutes indecent exposure.

Even so, the blandness and predictable stereotypes thrown up by the red carpet have proffered some useful tips. Although I'm not counselling a full-on swan-sized break from the norm, it is always a pleasure to see a short cocktail dress in the midst of all those goddess-aspirants at the Oscars, even if the fashion assistant does then stick a caption on it dismissing it as 'very off trend'. Similarly, a nice bright colour is a pleasure to glimpse among all the pastels and faded metallics. Ditto for a simple flat Alaïa ballet pump alongside all the beaded Jimmy Choos. Reese Witherspoon and Sofia Coppola are the modern icons of this and proof that 'quirky' need not be synonymous with 'on a hiding to full on senility, bless their bonkers ruffled socks'. It means 'pleasingly and prettily original' and don't ever let anyone tell you otherwise as it is commonly used as a grating insult against any woman who dares to voice or dress like she has an opinion. So the lesson from the red carpet is that looking a little different is a beautiful thing and God bless the celebrities for selflessly proving this by going the opposite way. Only the beige go beige.

Ruffles, *from French ingénue to Bozo the clown*

A tricky one, ruffles. A lot of women love them in the misguided belief they add a bit of 'fashion' to a garment – 'fashion' in this instance refers to any detail, no matter how ugly, that is introduced so as to, as your camp uncle might say, 'jazz up an outfit'. Beading, tassels and superfluous lace-ups also fall comfortably into this category.

Certainly, a bit of a ruffle is not necessarily the most offensive item a woman can have in her closet (slogan T-shirts avowing the wearer's attractiveness easily beat the comparatively harmless frill) and, in fact, some have been used to beneficial effect. Chanel, for example, is a label that has long mined the ruffle in its successful marketing of the French ingénue look to trust fund kids and rich old ladies around the world. But note, here the fussiness of the ruffle is actively sought in order to achieve Chanel's often cartoonish style.

Your feelings towards this style pretty much depend on whether the Audrey Tatou film *Amélie* made you want to dance out of the cinema and hand out daisies to strangers on the street, or run out of the auditorium and rip off your own head in order to get the overwhelming ocean of vomit out of your body just that little bit faster.

Ruffles are – in a very tenuous way, admittedly – like sugar: ration yourself to just the right amount and you're on to a sweet little winner; get carried away and you will gag on your own self-created saccharine mess. This tends to happen when they are used superfluously, such as around collars, which will make you look like a clown, a medieval court jester or Queen Elizabeth I, none of which, in terms of being a good daily look, is exactly a keeper. Instead, they need to be given a purpose and if you think ruffles can't have a purpose, well then, you are underestimating the power of fashion, o ye of little faith.

The most common breeding ground for ruffles is probably down the front of blouses, alongside the buttons. This actually isn't such a bad way to sneak them in and is a clever means of drawing attention to your bust in a faux-modest, oops-have-you-noticed-my-well-shaped-bust-well-I-never-intended-that-to-happen way. But make sure the ruffles are narrow to avoid the clown factor and just as blouses shouldn't generally be worn by anyone further down the alphabet than a C cup (see *Blouses, not so librarian now, are they?*), blouses with ruffles should not be favoured by anyone over a B cup unless you want to look like a walking heart rate monitor turned skew-whiff.

A skirt or dress hemmed with a wide (small would be pointless as people would not notice it), loose ruffle works in the same way as a puffball or A-line skirt in that it will make your legs look proportionally narrower yet without the paedo chic quality those two stylistic tricks can often bring.

Similarly, ruffled cuffs on blouses and dresses give one's hand a daintily ladylike look, even when you drag your cuff through a dish of hummus at a cocktail party and have to spend the rest of the evening with hands fringed by mulched chickpeas. Plus when you wave them about you can pretend you're Byron, mid-opus, an all too rare side-effect in the world of women's clothing.

And that, pretty much, is it. Anything else just becomes fashion chintz.

Sex and the City, *what it gave us in terms of fashion and what it didn't*

W ith the glorious exception of *Grumpy Old Men*, no TV programme has ever illustrated more truthfully human relations and modern malaise than *Sex and the City*. No, of course we all don't have that much sex and of course we don't have that much money, but for God's sake, it's an American sitcom – expectations of 'gritty realism' are a better indicator of your own naivety than that of the programme makers.

In terms of its depiction of fashion, it surpassed them all. Here were four women who lived on their own and earned their own money. Yet despite spending at least twenty minutes of every episode discussing where they were next going to get some, they never dressed for men. Yes, at least two, mainly one, of them did dress like total sluts in body-clinging Ungaro (Samantha) and nude Gucci (Carrie), but judging from the contented looks on their faces when they caught their reflections, this was more for themselves than anyone else. Sartorial masturbation, if you will. In any case, for all the praise the show's stylist Patricia Field accumulated for her impressive makeover of Sarah Jessica Parker, from aquiline-nosed B-lister to fashion doyenne, the fact is that most of the time Carrie looked really, really, really silly. To boys, that is – the girls, however, loved her. Let's see, there were the Chanel leggings, the de la Renta couture ball dress, the Juicy Couture playsuit, the giant corsages – these are not men-pleasing clothes. Heck, there was even a whole episode based on Carrie refusing to throw out some revolting feathered Cavalli top, even though her boyfriend was threatening to dump her unless she made some wardrobe room. Rather triumphantly, she kept both the top and the boyfriend. To be honest, purely from an aesthetic point of view, she probably should have ditched the jumper, but, hey, at least she was having fun. So for all the guff about the allegedly shockingly anti-feminist nature of this show it actually was anything but: *Sex and the City* was about working women who loved their jobs, dressed for themselves in supernaturally bright colours, had more fun together than they did with any man and lived vaguely surreal lives whose day-to-day plotlines bore only the shadow of a resemblance to reality. Yet unless 'anti-feminist' has somehow come to mean 'occasionally sleeps with a man' it's hard to see what the problem is. Just look at the above checklist: this show was basically an extended American version of a Pedro Almodovar film.

What it didn't give us was much in between. You either are a fashion obsessive and wear $1,200 dresses to lunch on Sundays (Carrie, Samantha, Charlotte) or you dress like a butch lesbian (Miranda). Nor did we get much on the downsides of fashion (feeling fat, feeling broke, feeling generally pissed off). But like I already said, this was a fantasy, and American, and a TV show, and Mike Leigh was presumably busy.

Its only real fault was the character of the *Vogue* editor played by Candace Bergen who fulfilled the kind of weary stereotypes we have come to expect from the film world about people who work in fashion (see *Films about fashion and why they are all (mainly) rubbish*). Another, albeit non-fashion related, criticism was why Carrie had to end up with the tedious, philandering Mr Big who had never done anything but make her unhappy. I'm not saying she should have ended up miserable and lonely, but perhaps on her own with new prospects on the horizon. If the whole point of the show was to depict independent women shaping life to their own making, then this 'happy' ending was dismayingly conventional.

But, that aside, this show did more to remind women that fashion was for them as opposed to any of the schlubby guys that occasionally come into one's life than any movie, magazine or TV show has ever done before. Mrs Bueller, hats off.

Shorts, *and why they're great*

 *Y*our opinion of shorts will generally depend on two factors: how keen you are on getting out the legs, and whether or not you lived through the eighties. If the answers to the above are, respectively, 'very' and 'yes, but I was too young to remember them' then you will almost certainly be more receptive to the style.

At some point in every woman's life she will have to ask herself that crucial question: is it all about the tits or the legs? In other words, would she do better focusing her sartorial efforts on showing off the top or the bottom half? For those who fly the flag for the latter option, shorts are the saving grace. They let you show off your legs without risk of flashing one's knickers or, worse, tights' gusset, with the added benefit of extra warmth. However, those who lived through the eighties will possibly find it hard to return to a garment that caused them so much mental trauma when it was worn by George Michael two sizes too small. Even some youngsters ignorant of this noble lineage (truly, today's young have no sense of history) might be a little nervous at dressing like they're en route to a seventies disco. For these cautious souls, the city shorts were invented.

The name 'city shorts' should give away some of the garment's inherent problems. Be wary of any piece of clothing with a name that very deliberately evokes a mood or demographic because any garment that needs some kind of contextualizing in order to look good is a garment that should probably be rejected. Think of all those designer bags that are, rather bizarrely, given names (Paddington, Roxy, etc., ad flipping nauseum), think Mary Jane shoes, think Peter Pan collars, think kitten heels, for God's sake. Sometimes this is not a problem. Prom dresses, for example, are quite clearly based on dresses that used to be worn to American high school proms. But the term 'city shorts' smacks strongly of retailers trying to give some kind of glamorous, modern edge to something that actually looks, to the untrained eye, like a leftover from a local panto. 'These shorts,' the name audibly pleads, 'are worn by the kind of glamorous people who stride the pavements with professionally blow-dried hair, their shades in place, making all sorts of

exciting appointments via the BlackBerry while en route to lunch at Shoreditch House with darling Charles and Nigella. Buy them and you'll get a bit of that action, too, you suburban slob.'

Having said all that, city shorts are not a bad design. They are very comfortable, modest and surprisingly fun to wear, in a novelty value kind of way. But you do run the risk of being mistaken for one of the Krankies and that is a risk no woman really needs to take on a daily basis.

As for winter shorts, the recently resurrected trend for thick wool shorts worn over cashmere tights, this, again, is strongly dependent on how clearly you remember the eighties. It's a look that is jolly fun to wear but, to anyone over the age of thirty-five, will make you look like one of Mel and Kim's backing singers. The triple layer of knickers, tights and shorts can make you feel like you're wearing a chastity belt but, on the plus side, does keep you warm on cold winter nights, and for the leg-flashing lady, so used to winter overexposure, this is a rare sensation indeed.

Signature *style*

The concept of a signature style is, at first, quite an appealing one. In the fashion world, it carries intimations of a woman with such strongly defined aesthetic tastes that she is not to be swayed by the flotsam of trends passing in the seas of time as opposed to, as cynics might sneer, a complete dearth of imagination and inability to conceive of more than one style of dress. You might think that the fashion world would be quite antipathetic to such madness, seeing as it spends a great deal of its time trying to convince the masses of the crucial nature of each passing trend. But, in a depressing *Rules*-type way, fashion folk, and particularly fashion designers, are fascinated by people who pay no attention to their commands. Well, some people anyway, because it should be stressed at this point that wearing a tracksuit three days on the trot, or still clinging on to last season's cropped jacket trend due to lack of awareness of its now passé nature do not count as signature styles. A true signature style has to be fashion aware, consciously cultivated and either very expensive or very uncomfortable. This ensures that absolutely no one else will dress like you, which is quite a crucial factor in the fashion-attention-grabbing game.

The exception to this rule is when a designer suddenly decides that the look of the signature style lady is just so fabulous that his next collection will be inspired by her, marketing her look to the masses. This is definitely permissible because if there's one thing better than being lauded for your personal style it's being dubbed 'a muse'.

Dita von Teese (retro male fantasy) and Rachel Feinstein (surreal fifties housewife) have inspired various designers' collections, perching contentedly in the shows' front rows as a bunch of underweight teenage models walked past wearing the same outfit as them. An experience most women would describe as being their vision of hell, but these ladies seemed to take it on the well-powdered chin. This muse thing does mean, of course, that when the designer has heartlessly ransacked our lady's wardrobe and then moved on to the next woman to pillage – Wallis Simpson, maybe, or Louise Brooks, dead muses being so much less high maintenance than live ones – the signature style woman's look inevitably is going to look irredeemably last season. But like a young wench who has been ravished then abandoned by the town's young bounder, she can console herself with the memories of when she was the centre of his focus, when Anna Wintour would nod at her at parties and her name – O glory days! – was in bold type on the party pages in glossy magazines in dentists' offices across the land. Now, though, she can only put that little pillbox hat on her head again, give her face an extra pat of powder and face the world with a fixed smile and let them all murmur admiration that she's still working that fifties look when the rest of us, obviously, have moved on to the eighties.

No matter what though, once your signature style has been generally recognized and duly celebrated you can find gratification with the thought that at least you once were part of the noble pantheon of 'style icons'. Talitha Getty. Grace Kelly. Coco Chanel. Lauren

Hutton. Audrey/Katharine bloody Hepburn. Rare is the year that passes without one of these ladies being named as a designer's 'inspiration' (see *Fashion speak*) that season due to their 'timeless iconic look'.

This concept of a style icon is actually an unexpectedly heartening one because – unusually in fashion, or in the modern world in general, for that matter – one doesn't necessarily need to be young to be one, or even need to be the least bit attractive. You just need to have a signature style that is so strong and constant it basically works like a loud and very belligerent argument, persuading people that it must be right out of sheer forcefulness and repetition. Diana Vreeland, the nasally blessed fashion editor of *Harper's Bazaar* from 1937 to 1962 and then editor of American *Vogue* from 1963 to 1971, is the ultimate example of this. A self-described ugly woman with a voice never once described as melodic, she is still revered as a fashion icon thanks to her penchant for Chanel suits, oversized jewellery and vampirically red lipstick and nail polish. She is the proof of fashion's occasionally democratic nature – a surprising result from one of the greatest snobs in fashion history, who once sniffed, 'What do I think about the way most people dress? Most people are not something one thinks about.'

For the rest of us mere mortals, there is a kind of watered-down signature style that most of us can and, indeed, do manage on a daily basis, which is called 'personal style'. This refers to the kind of clothes that you tend to wear in general: for example, if you are more of a jeans lady than a frock one then jeans are your 'personal style'. Yes, most people would simply call this 'having your own taste' but that doesn't sound quite as good. There are definite benefits to this 'personal style' thing. For a start, it makes it very easy for your friends to buy you presents. It also saves shopping time as a jeans lady would know never even to bother going into Miu Miu while the dress woman would rather carve out her eyeballs than bother with APC.

On the downside, it does mean you will spend your life hearing people say, as they pick up something in a shop that is pretty much guaranteed to be hideously ugly, 'That's so you.' This is a very annoying way of saying, 'That's so like something else that I think I have seen you wear before and would never, not in a million billion trillion years, ever consider wearing myself, and nor would anyone else.'

Moreover, your wardrobe also tends to be quite limited and you'll realize one evening that while you might have an extensive collection of round-toed high heels, you have absolutely no strappy sandals, which are the only kind of footwear that will go with the dress you bought that afternoon for the party you're due to arrive at in forty-five minutes. This is quite annoying too.

So look deep within your soul, ask yourself if, maybe, you're just hiding behind this personal style thing out of fear, neuroses, unconscious copying of your mother or just downright laziness and then get out there, girlfriend, and buy those strappy sandals. Cue triumphal end of credits music. *Chariots of Fire*, possibly.

Sizing, *the non-existent myth*

W hen the subject of size comes up it's hard not to come over a little bit atheist because this is a God that empirically, emphatically, irrefutably does not exist. And yet billions of women bow down to its altar daily, basing their mood, day and general sense of self on what this false God tells them that morning. Able to fit in the size 10 trousers today? Hurrah, life is sweet, you shall skip on down the street to the bus stop, patting small children on the head and waving jauntily to the newsagent, as if you were starring in a Judy Garland musical. Can't even get them over your lower thighs? A cloud as dark as pitch swamps your horizon, you are filled with self-loathing and self-disgust, you slump miserably into that weird muumuu your great-aunt left you and you cancel that lunch with your best friend you'd been looking forward to all week because you have decided never to eat again for the rest of your life (until later that afternoon when you eat two packets of biscuits because what's the point? You'll never be thin, may as well embrace the fatness, at least the Hob Nobs love you, etc., and so on).

The seemingly unshakable tendency of so many women to define themselves by their body shape has long since been transferred on to the numerical sizing system. Certainly, the system does lend itself to this, as the obsession with being a perfect 10, in both senses of the term, suggests. It is far easier to think of one's body shape as a 12, or whatever, than to bother faffing about with the scales every morning, particularly since those numbers have somewhat lost their power to tyrannize now that every woman's magazine soothingly assures its readers that the scales 'lie' due to muscle weighing more than fat – a reassuring tenet, to be sure, when you see that dial moving upwards, even if the most exercise you've done in a month is step up on to the scales.

Sizing also has a masochistically appealing suggestion of judgement, as though one were on *Eurovision* and watching the judges hold up their numbered placards: 'Eight! Congratulations! You are the ABBA of the competition!' 'Sixteen – loser! Back of the class with Gemini!' That sizes alter between designers and stores compounds this sense: Armani and Zara might love you but Paul Smith and Mango just trample on your self-worth every time. Surely everyone knows a woman (possibly the one in the mirror's reflection) who rules out even looking in whole stores simply because the sizing there is upsettingly stringent. Some cynically witty mouths have wisecracked that a large part of the appeal of Gap is that it uses American size numbers which are four lower than British ones. Thus, a size 12 is magically rendered into an 8 as soon as she walks under that blue-and-white sign, even if she did have two Toffee Crisps for lunch.

Yet this is precisely the point: sizes alter between shops and designers because there are no stipulations about what the measurements are. As everyone knows, one store's size 10 is another's 12. Thus, just because a dress says you are size 10 does not mean you are a size 10 because a size 10 does not exist. It is just a number the designer stuck into a randomly measured garment. To an extent, this does make sense: a woman who shops mainly at Armani probably will be of a slightly different body type than the one who more frequently goes to Topshop, and we'll get back to that in a second. But what doesn't make sense is how, even though every woman knows that sizes are not immutable, they still quail at their perceived power.

Designers have been able to use this fluidity of sizes to their advantage, but in interestingly different ways. On the one hand, you'd think it would be quite a clever wheeze for a designer to make their sizes as big as possible, thereby appealing to the numerically sensitive and, unsurprisingly, quite a few designers have done just that. But on the other, just as fashion magazines seem to think that the classier they are, the skinnier the models inside should be, so some designers indicate their brand image aspirations by making their sizes as small as possible, suggesting that their customers are from the fashionably neurotic demographic.

The high street is a slightly different issue. Unlike most designers, high street stores need to bear in mind that a large majority of their customers are teenagers and, thus, their sizes do have to be a little smaller, purely because otherwise they would have to put negative digits on some of their inside labels, so this does have an understandable sense of logic to it. Nonetheless, it does seem a bit tough on the adult high street shopper as it basically suggests that one has to pay higher prices in order to buy clothes with numbers inside that don't send you wailing and keening to the nearest trauma unit.

So although size numbers should not be seen as deeply affecting comments on your personal appearance, they should, nonetheless, be taken pretty personally. Because if size numbers define the store's self-image, then a store whose sizes seem to be so angrily unwelcoming is a store that is basically saying it doesn't want you as a customer. And you should respond in kind with a spin on your heel and your purse remaining tucked inside your whatever-sized jeans.

Sunglasses, *the meaning of*

*F*unnily enough, there once was a time when sunglasses were merely glasses to be worn in the – ooh, what was it? What's the word we're looking for here? Oh yes – sun. Yet these little darkened spectacles are a true testament to the strength of sartorial semantics, the (deep booming voice) power of fashion and (slightly quieter voice) the intriguing mentality of those who work in it.

During the course of the twentieth century sunglasses became the symbol of, pretty much in this order, the rich, the famous, the cool, the psychotic. In regards to the first, this was because in the pre-Easyjet era only rich people could afford to jet off to Capri with darling Miffy, Biffy and Squiffy for the summer to hang about on Jiffy's yacht, the *Tiffy*.

Then the famous got on to this shades thing, ostensibly to preserve their much-vaunted 'privacy', although seeing as sunglasses are now so synonymous with celebrity that there are some folk who would probably be unrecognizable without them (Elle 'aviator' McPherson, Nicole 'owl' Richie, Bo 'coloured' no), this argument doesn't really work so well any more.

No matter, once they became signifiers for wealth and fame sunglasses inevitably became symbols of coolness, seeing as these two states of being are the pinnacle of our collective life ambition.

With unexpected conservatism on the film industry's part, these outward shows of cool bad boy behaviour became easy wardrobe shorthand for baddies, usually trying to kill George Clooney.

But they also are as much of a cliché for people who work in fashion as Marlboro Lights. Seeing as most fashion people channel any tendencies to psychosis into compulsive shoe shopping and talking in non-sequiturs ('Eighties! Essential!') it would seem we're back to the first three meanings.

There are several possible explanations for what's going on here. First, because the fashion industry is, at heart, a big business about playing dress up it has so stunted the emotional maturity of all those who work in it that they still operate under the teenage mentality that refusing to make eye contact automatically makes you the coolest kid in the playground. Similarly, they cling on to the wealth and fame associations, both being definitely venerated in their industry seeing as it is those two demographics that are able to afford their clothes.

Next, that it makes them look ever so jet-setty, like they have to fly at a moment's notice to Jamaica for that shoot with Natalia before meeting up with J-Lo in Beverly Hills that they just don't even have a second to take off the shades, never mind that, thanks to Stelios, travel has lost its air of both exclusivity and glamour.

And making a brief nod back to the psychotic factor, there is no denying that hiding one's eyes does cause onlookers unease. This is very good. Although fashion is ostensibly about the pursuit of beauty, it does venerate certain looks not generally considered desirable in the outside world. Frailty comes to mind first here, but scariness is definitely on up there. This is partly to keep out outsiders by making fashion look much more complicated than it arguably actually is: if it were (blatantly) just about pretty dresses, why then, anyone would think (realize) they could do this lark. But it's also simply a career move. Whereas big city bankers might steal one another's clients and go on competitive drinking sprees in overpriced west London clubs, people in the fashion industry face down up and coming rivals by making themselves look as fearsome as possible – well, as fearsome as you can in a ladylike Chanel suit.

Sunglasses are also very useful for covering dark circles if one has been out a little too late with Kate and Lindsay and, like, everyone important at le Baron in Paris doing – oh God, you couldn't even imagine what they were doing. Even better, sunglasses are brilliant at suggesting that this is what you were doing even if, in fact, you just stayed up too late in your hotel room watching *Larry King Live* on CNN. Thus, they become metasuggestive. And you thought fashion was a shallow, single-layered affair.

Similarly, sunglasses might be very good at covering eyes purpled by recent cosmetic treatments, they are therefore even better at suggesting you've recently had something 'done', this now being something to vaunt as it proves your dedication to the cause.

And, finally, they mean you never run the risk of squinting which, you know, causes crow's-feet.

And so, to sum up, they make you look cool, they make you look rich, they get you attention because people think you might be famous and they might possibly stop wrinkles – frankly, it's a wonder the fashion world hasn't put them up for sainthood.

As for what you do with them, this, too, is fraught with vital semiotic signs that one must learn in order to avoid Fashion Death. Unless you are a yah-yah-ing, white-jeans-wearing, honey-tressed Sloane, they must never be worn on top of your head. This conveys the following messages: first, not only that you wish you were still on the King's Road circa 1987 when you could wear an Alice band in peace without fear of mockery, but also that you are a coward as you refuse to accept this truth and are opting out with a weak Alice band compromise (see *Hair accessories, gimmicks for reluctant adults*) or, two, that you think you are so famous that you need your specs at just a moment's notice in case a member of the – ewwww! – general public dares to invade your personal forcefield. So keep them on at all times, except when you go inside unless you are in a manufactured boy band video, in which case they are a key part of your wardrobe to try to convince fans that you are actually Quite Hard. When you must, tragically, remove them from your visage stick them in your handbag: folding them up and sticking them in your front pocket makes you look simultaneously like your dad on holiday and the president of a minor principality, two images one would not have thought possible to evoke at the same time, but such is the power of the sunglasses.

In terms of sunglasses style, the most gripping development in recent years has been the rise of the oversized sunglasses. This trend was started by the celebrity stylist Rachel Zoe, the woman who single-handedly made people think seventies kaftans were cool and Nicole Richie was glamorous and somehow, even more impressively, combined the two. The genius of oversized sunglasses is that they carry intimations of old school diva glamour (read: you can behave like a total bitch but people will forgive you because you look so fabulous); they have vintage store associations even if now they are so popular that most modern designers and high street stores make them; and they make your face look so small as to be – reeeesult! – malnourished. With such obvious attractions they have become the inevitable prop of every aspiring starlet and wannabe celebrity. Certainly, larger glasses are more flattering but the trend for ones so big that they all but make it impossible to eat (and again, reeeesult!) is rather akin to the theory that thin is in developing into the current situation where teenage models are dropping dead from heart failure. In other words, an idea taken a little bit beyond its originally intended meaning.

Aviators are for someone either whose heyday was in the eighties and they cling on to the memories – hence their popularity among ageing models and Sloanes – or who has an impressively impermeable and possibly subconscious veneration of Tom Cruise, the early years, i.e. the midlife crisis man and middle-aged gay men.

Coloured and decorated frames are just great for those who willingly describe themselves as 'a bit wacky'. They are also fabulous for squeezing on some extra logo names or Pucci swirls should you feel that your Balenciaga Lariat bag just isn't packing the sufficient amount of bling that day. This is perhaps the only instance in which these two demographics overlap.

Impermeably black ones are for spies, bodyguards, celebrities and fashion journalists. The first two use them to not be noticed and the other two use them for precisely the opposite reason. In this sense, black sunglasses are both an ambidextrous and bisexual accessory.

Alternatively, you could bypass the whole issue by taking tips from singer Loudon Wainwright III. Loudon may have been criticized by his children Rufus and Martha for his shortcomings as a father, but what the man lacks in paternal skills he more than makes up for in his sunglasses nous and hey, what's more important? So when you're standing in Harvey Nichols torn between buying a pair of gold embossed Cavalli shades with a tiny gold viper carved on the stems or a pair of even more geometrically ornate ones by Tom Ford, perhaps hum the following couplet to yourself from Loudon's song 'Grey in LA': 'Yeah, it might feel like fun when you're sporting sunglasses, but really you're just one more fool.'

Thin knits

*T*hin knits, baby! That's where it's happening these days! Eagle-eyed readers might espy the inherent contradiction in this concept, but, first, to the advantages. Ladies – and this style is one primarily for the ladies – like to be warm. But many don't want to disguise their charms wholesale, as anyone who has driven through an English town on a winter's Friday night knows. But even those who don't fancy risking hypothermia for the sake of heading out to All Bar One in a miniskirt mid-January generally don't want to resemble David Starsky, he of *Hutch* fame, burrowed beneath a giant cardigan. Hence the thin knit which, Marmite-ishly, gives coverage but not in great quantities. Yes, it is a bit sexier to be able to glance at just that hint of skin beneath an otherwise innocuous long-sleeved top and, yes, thin-knit tops have been a boon for the layering (see, yes, *Layering, the whats and the hows of*) trend. But seeing as knits are supposed to be about keeping you warm and the prefix here suggests they won't exactly do the job brilliantly, you do need to buy and then wear at least three at a time, if only not to expire from the cold. Sometimes, you really have to give the fashion industry credit for the ways they find to get people to spend that little bit more money.

Not that the fashion world now denigrates the chunky knit, of course, as seen in the cable-knit oversized jumpers by Stella McCartney and Chloé that are woollier than the whole of Wales. These (the jumpers, not Wales) have lovely connotations along the lines of snuggling down with one's boyfriend (boyfriends being much cooler than husbands, of course) in front of a big open fire in one's enormous but, you know, cool country pile in Shropshire or perhaps a chalet somewhere in France. So, to recap: thin knits – good, in a flash the flesh in a modest if frostbitten way; chunky knits – good in a suitably aristo setting. Isn't it nice how fashion can see the positives in everything? Let the cash tills ring in the new financial year!

Tights *and the pleasures of a chastity belt*

There are tights ladies and there are stockings ladies and the latter are simply wrong. Even leaving aside the silliness of their garment of choice, which we shall elaborate upon shortly, the criticisms they make of tights are – now let's see, how would Anna Wintour put this, ah yes – boneheaded.

First, they claim that tights are 'unsexy'. This accusation is predicated on the theory that sexiness is dependent on gynaecological access, an idea that is desperate, overly graphic and utterly, utterly ridiculous. Sexiness, wiser types have said for centuries, is all about suggestion, which really means, when it comes to clothes, ease of removal, hence the superior sexiness of a dress over a skirt and top combo. And perhaps with the exception of a bathrobe, it's hard to think of many things easier to wiggle off than a pair of tights. Stockings, on the other hand, have all these fiddly clips that twist up your knickers and when the clips snap on inconvenient body parts, well, let's just say that an element of surprise is not always a stoker to passion's flame.

Nor, while we're at it, are red marks around your thighs from where the stockings have been squeezing into you, whereas tights, oh blessed contraption, make you look as smooth as a late-night DJ's voice. Yes, it may be the classic male fantasy to see a woman in stockings, but the key word there is 'fantasy'. At no point has any man ever lain back in bed and thought: 'Oooh, you know what really gets the old motor going? Seeing a nice pair of thigh muffin tops. Oh, baby!' And if he did, he's probably the psycho from *The Silence of the Lambs* who throws women into pits but keeps his yappy little dog well-groomed. There's a lesson in there. Very deep in there, admittedly.

Next, the nonsense about tights being 'unsanitary'. Quite how anyone can maintain the argument that an extra layer of protection is less sanitary than exposure to all and sundry has never fully been made clear to the author. Moreover, having to fiddle about every time you need to go to the loo doesn't exactly sound like the most hygienic of ways to spend your day.

Finally, that tights are somehow 'claustrophobic'. Good God, woman, do you normally go commando? And you whinge about tights being unsanitary?

All women have felt the fear and, in some cases, the reality of walking around with their skirt tucked into the back of their knickers. Standing at the bus stop when your garter clip snaps, leaving your stocking pooling around your ankle and then trying to re-fasten it without being arrested for lewd behaviour while your fellow commuters snigger with undue pleasure is pretty much just as humiliating. And unless Sharon Stone in *Basic Instinct* is your personal icon, you can't cross your legs or even just reach your arms above your head when wearing stockings with a short dress. Tights, however, render high hems nigh on modest, but always get tights a size too big. This is not because you are actually fatter than you think but just for extra length in the leg so that your gusset doesn't hang out from below your skirt like an incontinence nappy.

Even more tedious than stocking propaganda is the idea that bare legs are the sexiest of all. Flesh may be more seductive than material, but flesh that is riddled with goosebumps due to undue exposure to the British winter is not, I would wager, most people's idea of sex on a stick. It's a look that is dependent on a taxi or chauffeured car lifestyle as opposed to standing around and waiting for the night bus.

Of course, as that great tights connoisseur George Orwell taught us all, while all tights are created equal some are more equal than others and the ones that are the legwear equivalent of Napoleon the ruling pig are lovely thick wool or cashmere ones. Unlike silly sheer ones, these simply get on and do what tights are meant to, namely, keep you warm and the world ignorant that you haven't shaved your legs since August. They make no apologies for being tights, as those awful flesh-coloured ones do, which end up giving you an intriguing peg leg look. They are also immensely more flattering than the black sheer ones that only ever looked good on the women in *LA Law* when they would perch on their boss's desk and switch their skinny legs about. And lest we forget, these women wore shoulder-padded blazers.

While tights should be celebrated, let's not get too carried away with the revelry. Grey, brown and black are the only acceptable colours – everything else is reserved for those whose highest ambition is to look like they've stepped out of Nintendo land.

Patterned tights were fun for about five minutes in 2002. Then one day we all woke up, collectively slapped our heads and realized we were walking around with polka dots on our calves and everyone sensible quite rightly chucked them in favour of plain or, at most, ribbed ones, which lengthen the leg and thus are very much for her pleasure ba boom boom and so on.

Fishnets, however, have lasted a little longer and just when they seem to be dying out they grab a last wheeze of oxygen around the office Christmas party season. At first there was something quite intriguing about their resurrection in that it looked like women were reclaiming a garment heretofore freighted with quite obviously negative associations.

But the problem with fishnets is their aspiration for cartoonish sexiness, tricked off with a half-hearted attempt at irony. Irony, like 'witty', may be an occasionally acceptable personality trait but is rarely a good look. Oversized fishnets were a little more interesting but one has to ask oneself whether making one's calves resemble the day's catch off a fisherman's trawler is really the look one wishes to pursue. They snag after one wear, they don't keep you warm and they leave criss-crossing red marks up your legs, making you look like you have caught some remarkable tropical skin disease. A potential conversation starter, yes, but possibly not the party look every little girl dreams of pulling off one day.

Toes, *and what the shape says about you*

*N*ot your own actual toes, of course. Except if your foot really is squared off, in which case you are, as all readers of Roald Dahl know, a witch, and you might want to bear that in mind, just for your own self-knowledge.

Dahl was, as ever, quite right: squared-off feet suggest an inhuman nature. Yet while the witches suffer terrible foot cramps attempting to disguise this physical deficit, some women today spend actual money on the reverse, buying shoes with squared-off toes. It really is the oddest thing. Look down at your little squared feet and ask yourself, what is it about this look that so appealed in the shoe shop? There are many times one might suffer the inevitable lifetime of limping for the sake of painful footwear (see *Heels*), but going for a witchishly squared-foot look is not, most would accept, a reasonable motive for such. And stop that nonsense about them being 'so much more comfortable'. Any shoe that does not follow the actual shape of your foot is not benefitting you in the slightest.

I fully concede that pointy-toed shoes are just as unacceptable as their dumpy squared counterparts, and maybe even more so because the wearer generally has adjectives of the 'sexy', 'vamp-ish', 'Linda Fiorentino' variety running through her mind, when she looks like a Bond villain with switchblade-concealing shoes. In fact, they simply look mean. Just look at the way Gillian McKeith's unfailingly pointed black boots peek out from beneath her black trousers and tell me if there is not something of the night going on here. And let's not even get into the theory about pointed shoes being 'leg lengthening': anyone who mistakes an elongated pointed shoe tip for being a long and lean thigh is obviously a person of irrelevantly limited intelligence.

Both the squared- and pointed-toe shoe work on the odd prin-ciple that they suggest your foot has a shape that everyone knows it doesn't. Yes, sometimes fashion does encourage this forced body reshaping (padded bras, control top tights, corset-style tops), but this is generally because onlookers could potentially be fooled into thinking that the wearer actually does have, respectively, globular breasts, a flattened stomach and an hourglass figure. No one, surely, would look at a squared or pointed shoe and think it's the actual shape of the foot inside, nor, one can only presume, would the wearer want them to do so. Yet while the similarly bizarre and semiotically incomprehensible shoulder pads have, happily, long ago been con-signed to the ever-growing pile of fashion embarrassments, still we plough on with this odd-shaped footwear.

Of course, to take this toe argument much further would result in arguing for diagonally shaped shoes, that being the shape of your foot and all, and that is probably too much of a leap as yet for the timorous pointed- and squared-toe masses.

The obvious compromise is the rounded toe. It is perfectly pretty in an innocuous kind of way, it suits every shoe style and – and listen up, square-ish die-hards – is comfortable. Now, the problem with the rounded toe is that, as proven by the plethora of upsetting high street ballet pumps (see *Ballet pumps, twee versus comfort*), it is unexpectedly hard to do well. It has to look delicate, ladylike, yet not too exaggeratedly Minnie Mouse. The ideal shape is like that of the top of a slightly wonky egg, with the high rounded tip to one side and then fanning downwards. Marc Jacobs and Chloé have perfected the style and some valued members of the high street such as Kurt Geiger have learned their curving lessons. It can look a little too girlish, but this is generally the fault of the shoe as opposed to the toe, so if you don't want to look like you work at Disney World, don't buy red polka dot Mary Jane high heels. A motto, perhaps, some women should have embroidered on the outside of their wallets.

Still, both the pointed and the rounded toe are preferable to the open toe and even its cheating compromise, the peep toe, simply because they are much less high maintenance. There is a rather sweet theory that open-toed shoes are sexier than their closed counterparts, and this probably is true, even if, seeing as the foot is not widely regarded as the sexiest part of a woman's anatomy, it does suggest that we haven't moved too far from the Victorian days of yore when piano legs were allegedly considered quite the hubbest of hubba. Certainly the open-toed strappy shoe is a remarkably useful piece of footwear because, thanks to its near invisibility, it is much more versatile and can be worn with pretty much any garment in your closet. However, a woman who wears open-toed shoes is a woman who has time and patience in her life for weekly pedicures, nightly foot moisturizing and a social life that tends to involve sitting decorously in glamorous bars in Ibiza with P. Diddy and Cameron Diaz.

The peep toe is deceptively just as demanding. Only one toe tends to be visible but for that very reason you'd better make sure that toe is up to scratch because all the attention will be on it. The peep toe has associations with fifties starlets, burlesque dancers and rather fabulously devil may care French women strolling down the piers in St Tropez. But one should never look for style guidance from a French woman: it would be like hoping to pick up some mental arithmetic tips from Stephen Hawking – some people are just made from a different, more instinctively rigorous model than the rest of the human species and, for a French woman, a weekly pedicure is probably up there with dog grooming in terms of obviously essential weekly appointments. In regards to burlesque dancers, they pre-sumably have bugger all else to do with their daytime hours other than schlep on down to the local nail salon while mentally deciding on which boa and corset combo to wear that night. And as for fifties actresses, well, maybe there wasn't that much else to do in the fifties other than get your nails done, seeing as cable TV hadn't yet been invented and all.

Topshop, *and how it changed the (fashion) world*

It is now too simplistic to describe the high street as fashion fast food compared to the haute cuisine one finds on Bond Street. Back in ye olde times of BT (Before Topshop) this might have been true, when the high street was best described with reference to Bart Simpson's favourite cartoon, *Itchy and Scratchy*. But then fash-ion dynamo, Jane Shepherdson, took over as brand director at Top-shop in 1998 and, funded by the wisely hands-off Philip Green, who owns the fashion conglomerate to which Topshop belongs, com-pletely changed the way Britain shops and sees fashion and, most of all, what customers expect from clothes in general.

Uniquely, Shepherdson realized that having a tight fashion

budget was no bar to having a brain: just because someone could only afford clothes with single or low double digit price tags did not mean they wouldn't realize when they were being fobbed off with tacky or just plain dull tat. Just by making the tiniest of adjustments – a bit of piping around the cuffs, say, or extra large buttons down the front, or a sexy scoop neck instead of the usual thoughtless high-neck style – makes the difference between generic and genius when it comes to fashion and it was Shepherdson who brought these in-expensive tricks to the high street, all of which were quickly picked up by the aspirants in her wake.

British folk have always taken a preening sort of pride in their frugality ('Central heating? Codswallop! Just put on an extra jumper, but mind you wait until mid-January in order to feel the benefit'), and so the idea that you could now get cheap stuff that was actually good, well, it was like gasoline on a low-burning fire, flaring up into a still burning national delight in boasting about how little one has spent on one's outfit.

In part, Shepherdson was helped by fortuitous timing. She came along just when fashion was starting to get younger. Labels such as Chloé, Stella McCartney, Miu Miu and, in particular, Marc by Marc Jacobs offered up some valuable tips on how to make young fashion look cool, such as, respectively, making pretty tunic dresses, slouchy jumpers, cute tweed outfits and brightly coloured basics.

And for a while, the high street floated happily on a wave of designer copies, with each season bringing rumours of the latest spot-on Chloé-esque dress to be found on the clothing rails of – of all places – Tesco, for example. This completely changed the way Britain saw fashion: no longer was it about snotty-faced rich people at charity dinners; now it had taken on a personal relevance. One had to pay attention to who made what so as to spot the dead-on copies and then experience the indescribable satisfaction of being asked whether your bag is from Chloé and to be able to answer, 'Kookai, actually.'

Yet precisely because the clothes were so cheap it now became acceptable not just to buy them but to pay attention to fashion in general. There is not a celebrity magazine or daily newspaper in this country that doesn't cover high fashion to some degree; when it was announced that the relatively little known Phoebe Philo was resigning from Chloé many of the broadsheets ran full-page articles. Thus, Topshop cleverly turned Britain's inherently prudent nature in on itself, making it one of the most fashionably clued-up countries in the world, with any twenty-something female worth her blonde highlights able to talk knowledgably about Marni tunics and Luella handbags but – and this is key – in a savvy, non-Paris Hilton manner because she knows that high expenditure is not an inherent sign of coolness. Quite the opposite, in a lot of cases.

Topshop, and soon the majority of the rest of the high street, dropped this ultimately quite reductive crutch and, like a baby bird, learned to fly out of the nest on their own. Some crashed to the ground, most soared upwards, still employing the lessons taught by Shepherdson, who left Topshop in 2006, to mass national dismay, by making clothes that suggest at least some thought went into them, as opposed to just churning out a bunch of badly fitted T-shirts that bag under the arms and are just that little bit too short so that the ol' muffin top is on general view.

The final triumph came when celebrities started to shop on the high street, as opposed to simply providing the template for the styles to be copied. There ain't nothing like seeing the blouse you picked up yesterday in Dorothy Perkins worn by a pop star being interviewed on TV to make one realize that the gap between celebrities and mere mortals is really more of a stream than a gulf. And when it was announced that Kate Moss was to design a collection for the store, well, not even Trotsky could have conceived of a better sign of the levelling out of society.

Of course, the high street is not perfect, and luckily for designers, never will be.

What it is very good at is making fun clothes (as well as making clothes themselves fun). Party dresses, cute tops, jeans, summer frocks, bathing suits, costume jewellery, casual jackets, shorts, miniskirts – these should all be bought on the high street. What it is less good at, unsurprisingly, is making clothes that require a bit more time, resources and skill than your average Chinese sweatshop worker has. Thus, good trousers, long-lasting winter coats, blouses, grown-up smart dresses, suits and proper jackets are not so great in the £50 and under outlets. Accessories, too, aren't necessarily the best of investments on the high street and are guaranteed to wheeze out and die long before those from a posher shop do. One could argue that, in fact, the high street is to blame for the incredible rise in prices in the luxury fashion market in recent years, particularly in regard to handbags. Designers realized that the only way to stay ahead was to make things too complex for the yappy little high street to be able to equal. Thus, handbags soon became laden down with gold chains, big padlocks, quilted leather and chain straps, none of which can be knocked off on the cheap without looking, well, cheap. Not only could the high street not compete here, but designer prices inevitably had to rise, too, in order to be able to maintain this level of complexity in their own wares. A similar state of affairs began to happen with designer clothes and the suspicious rise in popularity of embellished garments on the catwalk. A dress covered in mirrored shards and Perspex pieces may dazzle when done well; do it on the cheap and you look like a bathroom in a Moroccan B & B. People simply expect more from designer clothes these days now that we know that, actually, it isn't that hard to make a vest top that actually fits or a summer dress splashed with some beautiful pattern.

And so, Topshop ultimately made fashion both more and less accessible and Britain both more parsimonious but also more profligate about clothes. Foreign fashion journalists might not bother coming to Britain for London Fashion Week, but they do come to pick up cheap dresses at Oxford Circus. And somehow, in a country that turned punk into haute couture thanks to Vivienne Westwood, such a contradictory kind of legacy seems endearingly apt.

Trench *coats*

The trench coat, like the pencil skirt, little black dress and 'a proper handbag', is one of those items fashion magazines always say one simply has to own as part of one's grown-up, basic wardrobe, but actually just makes you feel like you're trying to pretend you're in some terrible French film. At least the pencil skirt et al have rather glamorous precedents – respectively, Deneuve, Hepburn and Birkin – whereas few have aspired to look like a detective with an 'Allo 'Allo accent. This veneration of the trench coat is an interesting example of the Law of David Jason: if something simply hangs around for long enough it will eventually be applauded as 'a classic'. But the fact is, like the pencil skirt, the trench coat doesn't suit all that many women. It's a coat – but not very warm; it's for outdoor wear – but shows up dirt like billy-o; it's a similar colour to a lot of women's skin tone – which will just make you look

jaundiced. And yet, and yet, on it lingers, haunting the pages of fashion magazines like an old smell of cabbage in a dead relative's flat.

Admittedly, the trench coat can look quite chic on some women. Kate Moss comes to mind, glamorous French women follow on her heels. But the former would look decent in a dress made of cellophane, which, in fact, she really did wear once. And the latter are foreign so we just accept their peccadillos. But this is the truth of trenches: like all clothing, they suit some people and not others. Amazing, n'est-ce pas? So don't be fooled by this classic or, worse, 'staple' moniker. A magazine that describes a trench coat as a classic is almost certainly a magazine gunning for that Burberry advertising account.

Vanity, *the joys thereof*

W hen people knock fashion the most common criticism is that it's a vain, self-obsessed pursuit. But it's never been made wholly clear why fashion is denigrated as shallow when similarly aesthetically based industries like, say, cinema or art or theatre, are lauded as spiritually enriching. Those three also involve huge sums of money, attract appallingly egotistical people and tend to exclude anyone below the middle-class stratum. Yet if you spend an evening watching some poncey folk ponce about on a poncey stage, you are lauded for your cultural pursuits, whereas if you wile away a harmless afternoon admiring some pretty dresses in a shop, you are irredeemably self-indulgent. Retaliate with this argument and you will be accused of being 'facetious'. Being a fashion airhead, I'm unsure of the exact definition of this word, but I suspect it means 'annoyingly right'.

As for the argument that fashion is a hideous waste of hilarious amounts of money, my God, have you seen how much paintings go for these days? A Klimt for $73 million, wasn't it? Or have you checked out Tom Cruise's *nine*-figure paycheque for the coma-inducing *War of the Worlds*?

Let's not get into the hoary is-it-art-or-is-it-fashion debate, mainly because it's boring, but also because it becomes a bit of a red herring in that it suggests that fashion has to pretend to be Monet in order to be tolerated. Fashion produces no more personal dissatisfaction than watching Cameron Diaz on screen, is no less prone to whims and trends than the art world, and is usually a lot more fun than seeing *Hamlet* for the seventy-second time.

The fact is, feeling pride in one's appearance gives happiness and self-confidence. I concede that at times this does cross over into extremes resulting in quite the opposite, with women labouring under a lifetime curse of self-hatred and physical contortion, and this is very wrong. But it seems similarly anti-female to insist that in order to be a true feminist, one is not allowed to have any vanity. This is just a breath away from the old anti-feminist stereotype about hairy armpits and burlap trousers which has led to a current generation of girls loath to describe themselves as feminists in the belief that this makes them sound in favour of body hair as opposed to equal pay.

Patriarchal society or not, everyone likes to look good. Even Ann Widdecombe went blonde, and, as that example proves, this is not just about looking good for the boys – it's about looking in the mirror and having a little smile.

Here, one suspects, lies the potential nub of the anti-fashion prejudice. Good God, women doing something – just for themselves? Spending their own money? Women making themselves feel good about themselves rather than self-martyrishly chaining themselves to the sink and raising Lord Toffy Toff's children while he's off shagging his PA? An industry dominated by women? Dear God, cover your eyes, think of the children!

I concede that there is a difficulty in deciding whether something makes you feel better because you genuinely like it or because you are conforming to society's expectations of what you should look like. But perhaps we could all give one another credit at being able to figure that one out on our own. And look at it this way: it is a proven fact that you are more likely to get a job if you dress nicely. Object to the superficiality of this world all you like, but the fact is that the more women who look decent and feel self-confident, the more women there will be in good jobs so we can take over the world. And seeing as Germaine Greer is now otherwise engaged discussing the joys of the rabbit vibrator, I'd say *Vogue* is probably a better option these days than *The Female Eunuch*.

Velvet, *and why it should be banned*

*T*he problem with velvet is not so much about how it looks (although that certainly is problematic) but what it does. This is a fabric intrinsically associated with two subjects particularly prone to being laden with clichés – namely, elderly women and festive fashion. Seeing as the Queen provides the link to this Venn diagram, and, in fact, has long been partial to a bit of velvet, we may as well blame her.

To the older women first. With the exception, perhaps, of women who play the harp or sing in medieval music groups, there is not a female alive under the age of sixty who ever considers buying a velvet dress or, God save us, velvet trousers except in very specific circumstances, and we shall return to those in a tick (and if there is, there shouldn't be. This is a fashion book, OK? We deal in how the world ought to be.) Velvet is a fabric best reserved for, at most, covering a small side table in a National Trust house. Yet somehow, it has become ingrained in women's minds that this profoundly and garishly ugly material is what they should wear as they enter their seventh decade. It is clumsily heavy yet unflatteringly clingy and the way it changes colour tone when the pilling is rubbed the wrong way makes it look like it is covered with dribble stains.

Now, if older women actually liked it that would be fine – odd, but fine. But the uniformity of the point at which they start wearing it suggests that wearing velvet, like suddenly becoming partial to doilies or sporting headscarves, is something they do because they think that's how a mature woman should behave. The fact that clothing manufacturers seem to think so, too, and therefore get rid of all their velvet offcuts by flogging it off to the – snigger – oldies may have even more to do with it. But if there's one time in life when you shouldn't be embracing such unnecessary clichés it's when you get older. C'mon, you're still alive and kicking (albeit perhaps not as high as you used to) – just because Jaeger says you should now dress how you remember your granny doing doesn't mean that you have to or that you're now elderly and redundant. There's enough ageism out there without you conforming to its worst diktats. Get on down to Zara, ma'am, and find yourself a nice sharp jacket and blouse, wear them with your favourite trousers for walking the corgis and you might actually start to show your teeth when you smile.

Festive dressing is a major victim of enforced sartorial stereotypes. If sitting round for sevety-two hours with family members you never particularly liked, getting fat on food you definitely don't like and watching TV shows that nearly put you off the medium for life wasn't bad enough, somehow finding yourself wearing a bulky knitted jumper or head-to-toe red or, yes, something velvet will definitely dent your mood.

Quite when it became an accepted truth that one should wear really weird clothes at Christmas is not entirely clear. Possibly it coincided with the rise in the horror that is the office Christmas party in the eighties. Here is an event when people will suddenly be gripped by the desire to show how crazy and fun they are normally, beneath their PowerPoint-happy exteriors. All those across-the-floor crushes, long-term grievances and general repression nurtured throughout the year come to full flower in a cavernous room, filled with discarded and split plastic cups, watery white wine and the pulsating tune of (the now forever ruined) *Hey Ya!*

Velvet is a well-beloved fabric for a woman at an office Christmas party because, like, it's festive but also a bit sexy, in that it makes men want to stroke you, right? No, it makes men wonder why you're dressed up like the sofa at their in-laws'. For the male boss, a velvet waistcoat is the perfect thing for showing that they're as up for a bit of, chortle chortle, festive fun as the next Dire Straits fan.

As for the man in a velvet suit, ask yourself this, is a seventies lounge singer really what you reckon every woman dreams of bringing home to Mum and Dad one day? You're not Jarvis, get over it.

Vintage

*V*intage, schmintage – it's not the concept that bothers, it's the snotty-faced justifications behind its recent election to the top of the fashion pyramid.

Ever since people (a.k.a. Kate Moss) popularized vintage clothes about a decade ago her followers have come up with some rum old justifications for this trend:

1. 'Only vintage clothes fit my small shape.' As a modern lady with a modern body built by modern foods like Crunchy Nut Cornflakes and Bacardi Breezers, I have little truck with that.
2. 'They don't make clothes like they used to', which is as annoying and erroneous as saying something like 'TV has really gone downhill since the sixties.'
3. 'At least no one else will be wearing this dress at the party', a concern which would seem to display a really quite impressive lack of something called a sense of humour.

Vintage came into fashion basically when lots of models started wearing it, models being the only species on earth who have sufficient time to trawl through racks of dead people's clothes

to find the occasional nuggets, the funds to buy them, and the
bodies to make anything – even dead people's clothes – look
good. And as all good readers of *Heat* and *Elle* know, once a
model is spotted in something, that particular garment is obviously
A Good Thing. And there were, I fully concede, some rather
nice things unearthed: Kate Moss in a smashing yellow dress;
um, Kate Moss in a polka dot dress; er, Kate in a shimmering
gold minidress. And, you know, I'm sure there are plenty more
to be found. But really, who has time for all that digging through
piles of crap, all that rifling through jumbled rails, all those cold
mornings going to street markets and digging through bin bags?
Whatever happened to a good old-fashioned shop with everything labelled nicely and various sizes available? Yes, maybe that
does make me a brainwashed sheep but, you know what? I'm
a brainwashed sheep with a lot more free time on my hands.

Also, I'm not saying that a fair bit of modern fashion leaves something to be desired, but this is not quite the same thing as saying
everything old is good. For a start, you have to ask yourself why, if
this stuff is so good, has somebody given it away in the first place?
I've seen a pair of beaten-up old DMs that were going for £100
because they were 'early nineties originals'; I've seen tea-stained
H&M tops being dubbed 'original eighties'. Go on eBay and any
bit of old tat finds absolution in the label 'vintage'. What nice stuff
there was in the vintage market is now priced to such hilarious
levels that it somewhat undermines vintage's original image as being
the bohemian alternative. And we haven't even mentioned other
joys of vintage shopping, such as being sneered at by the vendor
for not recognizing that something was 'an original' (truly, the only
thing worse than a vintage fashion snob is a vintage fashion seller
snob); having to listen to the seller bark on about how Kate Moss /
Alexander McQueen / John Galliano gets all their stuff from them
(Kate Moss is the link between vintage sellers and drug dealers –
every single blessed person in both of those professions likes to

make scepticism-inducing claims to have had dealings with the young lady); realizing that every piece of vintage you've bought actually just makes you look like Miss Havisham and/or Bet Lynch, and having to quell the strong suspicion that you are being royally ripped off. Vintage shops often have an intriguing aversion to putting pricetags on their clothes. Possibly this is because their amazing wares accrue in value with every passing day. Possibly for some other reason, who really can say.

The truth is, there is a suspicious synchronicity between the moment when vintage became fashionable and the high street got good. I don't want to come over all Oliver Stone here but one can't help but wonder if the reason people started cooing over one-offs and overpriced seventies dresses is because the masses were suddenly able, for the first time in quite a while, buy decent clothes for themselves. Quick, quick! We have to find some way to make them feel that isn't quite good enough! I know! Let's tell them that the high street is manufactured tat whereas if you really want to keep it real you have to pay £700 for an Ossie Clark dress from Rellik! Yeah, baby – that's what I call staying grounded.

Volume, *and the ironic cruelty of the oversized cut*

W hen these balloon, pouffed, sack or whatever-euphemism-you-prefer shapes re-emerged this century it looked, at first, like designers had finally begun to realize that life does not stop at seven stone. Ah, glory be, customers cried! Clothes that one can wear when over a size 12 and not look like a sausage stuffed by an overenthusiastic factory worker! Dresses that don't crush one's ribs or collapse one's lungs! How fortunate are we!

In fact, voluminous clothes turned out to be even more fascistic about size than the tightest catsuit in Nancy dell'Olio's wardrobe. Just as clothes that appear to be from Miss Havisham's wardrobe

– oversized cardigans, Chanel-esque tweed jackets, pencil skirt suits – ironically look best on young women (ref Marc Jacobs and Chloé) simply because on anyone else they would look, well, old, so oversized clothes can only be worn on the very, very thin. Think of it this way: a sack-like dress on a twig-like woman emphasizes her twigginess due to the contrast between its bagginess and her bony legs. But a sack-like dress on a larger woman merely looks like that's the only thing she could fit into. This is what is known as a fashion tease: you think, at last, your needs have been recognized, only to then discover that it's all for someone whose needs are already well and truly catered for. It's like when the gorgeous boy at school starts to hang around with you for, you think, your fabulous sense of humour and encyclopaedic knowledge of eighties indie bands. But in fact, he's still getting off with the cheerleaders behind the sheds and just using you for a bit of idiosyncratic cred.

The one upside to this cruel twist of fashion fate is that this rule, in the main, is only apparent to those in the fashion world. To all the little people outside, it makes absolutely no sense at all because oversized clothes on skinny people merely make them look fragile and, outside fashion's vicious circle, fragility is not generally a look to be desired. However, the sharp twist in that tail is that, to most people, no one looks good in baggy clothes because, well, they're baggy. You can bandy about phrases such as 'Cristóbal Balenciaga's original sack dress' and 'très Paul Poiret' all you like but ultimately, unless onlookers have well and truly affixed their fashion goggles upon their twitchy little noses they will simply think you are wearing a sack, Paul Poiret be damned.

This is not to say that volume as a whole need be dismissed or that Ms dell'Olio had it right all along. It just needs to be used like salt, with a delicate and health-conscious pinch. So instead of a full-on sack, just wear a loose top and then, as a compromising nod to those who don't care about Balenciaga's original quasi-couture styles, narrow trousers or a similarly fitting skirt. Alternatively, you could go for a tight bodice-style top and then a puffed-out skirt, but many women tend to favour the former approach, partly because they feel a bit daft dressing like ballerinas when they're over twenty-five (unless they are actually ballerinas, of course, in which case, fair enough) and partly because many prefer to keep the area around their stomach hidden beneath soothing folds of fabric as opposed to cinching it in and thereby ruling out any possibility of eating that day. Thus it doesn't look like you are hiding beneath swathes of material to disguise the parts of you that you'd rather not be faced with every hour of the livelong day and cheekily flaunting your best assets (even if that is what you're doing) but rather that you're being ever so insouciantly modest and, by heavens, if that is how good her legs are, imagine what she has going on beneath that smock top! And going back to the earlier example for geriatric chic, it ultimately comes down to clever contrast: a Chanel-style jacket with a pair of jeans: good; a Chanel-style jacket with a Chanel-style tweed skirt: how many will be joining you for lunch at Le Caprice, Lady van eighties Throwback?

An interesting example of both of these rules combined was proffered up to the masses by a thankfully briefly lived trend mastermined by the remarkably successful celebrity stylist, Rachel Zoe. Between 2005–6. Zoe was the woman behind the curtain, controlling the unexpected fashion idolatry of the likes of Nicole Richie, Lindsay Lohan and other such cultural luminaries with her coining of a trend, brilliantly dubbed by *Tatler*, The Dead Socialite Look. This trend, as the name suggests, was inspired by socialites from the past such as Nan Kempner, Babe Palely and Gloria Guinness – women who actually managed to outsnob that ultimate über snob, Truman Capote. Charming women, one and all, thank heavens we continue to celebrate their legacy. Anyways, this look involved lots of old lady-ish tweeds, original vintage voluminous kaftans and billowing smock tops, all of which worked wonders to emphasize Richie's skinniness and wealth but, on anyone over seven stone and who cannot afford the Pucci originals, would make them look like Elizabeth Taylor, the Fortensky years. Thus, it managed to be both the most size-ist and class-ist trend yet coined and, for that alone, Zoe's sudden if brief position as the most influential stylist of her time is well deserved.

Yoga, *detoxes and other euphemisms for exercise and diets*

*E*ven the most adamant defenders of fashion will concede that, when it comes to women's bodies, in this business thin is always more desirable than fat. However, somewhere between the late eighties and the mid-nineties the words 'diet' and 'exercise' started to chime in a very off-key way. They just sounded, well, a little anachronistic, tacky, even. Which is odd because certainly being thin had not become either of those things: if anything, the thinness bar was being set still higher, or lower, or whatever, as the fashion ideal shifted from Cindy Crawford playing volleyball in a swimsuit to Kate Moss looking mopey in a vest and knickers in what appeared to be a crack den.

So if it wasn't the goal, it must have been the methods that were tarnishing. Et voilà, the emergence of detoxing and yoga, which are, respectively, morally superior dieting and stretching with an added dose of self-obsession.

Once detoxing and yoga, like their crucial accessory, the health food shop, were the embarrassing province of milky-faced, stringy-haired hippies who played wind chimes and had distasteful sex that probably involved a chant in praise of the power of the uterus. Now, however, their benefits were being celebrated by the most desirable sorts of people in town (i.e. models, actresses and the wealthy).

Other euphemisms that emerged included:

1. Looking after oneself
2. Going on a retreat
3. Getting healthy

Partly this was because of the growing concern in the media over the connection between the open-mouthed slavering veneration of thinness and eating disorders, and so fashionable sorts had to find codewords for their pursuit of visible bones that didn't sound quite so overt. Once, in a kingdom known as pre-1996, yoga and detoxing were about separating oneself from shallow, material worldly goods, so there is something very pleasing about how they have since been requisitioned as being the path to that well-known spiritual state, having a flat stomach.

The real reason for all this was because dieting and going to aerobics classes turned into victims of their own success, the classic casualties of market saturation. Dieting became redolent of daytime-TV-watching housewives, the coverline promises of weekly women's magazines and buckets of strawberry-flavoured meal-replacement powder sold in chainstore chemists. In other words, anyone could diet. Well, what's the point of that, then? It was all right in the eighties when diet and exercise brought to mind cool aerobics instructors in sexy leotards and high-flying businessmen taking power showers, but definitely not when it became about Rosemary Conley doing leg lifts on the covers of books sold in newsagents. And if the value of thinness, like being blonde, lies in its relative exclusivity, then it is VERY ANNOYING to see the great unwashed making the same kind of efforts as you to jump on this bandwagon.

Furthermore, to diet and exercise proves that you have to work at being thin. This is simply unacceptable. Fat has become a physical symbol of laziness, gluttony and, thanks to Gillian McKeith and her various television imitators, being lower class – the kind of yob who sits on the sofa watching Jeremy Kyle while eating a bag of Fritos, as opposed to dashing about town between one's acupuncturist and dinner with Sienna and Keira while snacking on an organic papaya. Thus, to admit that you have to make an effort to keep thin suggests that you are some kind of faker, a cuckoo in the nest of glamorous upper middle-class acceptability whose true nature is only barely kept at bay.

And speaking of class concerns, let us not forget that it is much more expensive to detox than to diet, a bunch of organic, ethically grown and harvested by happy workers cherries being a damn sight more costly than a tub of Slim Fast. Even though one could easily lose weight by shopping at a cheap supermarket, a fridge full of Lidl products, even if they include skim milk, fruit and water, is definitely less with it than a cupboard of Whole Foods' own brand. The latter also suggests that, you know, you care about what you put into your body, that you know about carcinogenics, pesticides and genetic modification, whereas anyone who shops elsewhere is an uneducated, *Daily Express*-reading dullard. Now, while you might have thought that putting so much effort and thought into one's every foodstuff bespeaks a life that is perhaps a little bit empty, this is to miss the undercurrent of class snobbery flowing strong here. As with the fuss about vintage shopping compared to contemporary clothes, to shop at organic markets requires more time and money than, as already said, just to go down the supermarket. Thus, a person who does so must (a) not have a very time-demanding job and (b) a steady flow of cash. Again, very desirable: to overtly work for one's cash suggests cuckoo-status. There is something of the student mentality here in that it is just not cool to say that you are making an effort with your studies, whereas just pulling out that First at the end of the year with minimal library time is what it's all about. Funnily enough, it is precisely the privileged, upper middle-class sorts who populate higher education who are the biggest supporters of this detox etc., attitude. Frankly, I blame it all on the Bodleian.

On a vaguely more positive note, all this detoxing and these yoga-class waiting lists are a rather endearing verification of our own, undeniable, unfightable, inherently lazy natures. On a purely mental level, it sounds less self-denying to tell yourself that you are detoxing as opposed to not eating chocolate for a week. Similarly, yoga, while potentially quite strenuous if you want to look like Madonna, is generally less of a faff than a circuit training class. Thus, they are a means to trick oneself into being thin, as though we'll wake up one morning and find ourselves with the lithe, lean body of a seventeen-year-old girl purely by means of a month of eating organic fruit'n'nut bars and doing cat poses. Really, it's actually quite sweet in a kind of childlike way. Here we are, all puffed up with pride about our medical advances, our knowledge about the world's origins and booking flights to the moon, yet we still think buying a £7.95 tub of aloe vera juice will somehow make us morally superior and painlessly thin, or that wearing something with 'skinny' in the name will endow us with the same quality, and that a bit of cheap dark plastic in front of our eyes will convince the world that we are very, very cool. To quote that well-known fashion commentator, Tiny Tim (have you seen his skinny legs? Like, beyond fabulous), God bless us, every one.

Acknowledgements

So many people to thank, so little desire to inflict a load of mwah-mwah acknowledgements on the reader. Oh well, tough luck.

And so, a big thank-you to: Ian Katz for everything; Katharine Viner and Merope Mills for maintaining a sorely tested belief that there might be some wheat despite all the chaff; Jess Cartner-Morley for being the best editor, inspiration and friend a lady could ever hope to find; Alexandra Shulman for endlessly appreciated support and encouragement; the two Kates in my life, Jones and Barker, the supersonic agent and editor and their respective entourages – Laura Sampson at ICM and Venetia Butterfield, Tom Weldon, Eleo Gordon, Ann Cooke and John Hamilton at Viking; Heather Schroeder at ICM and Hilary Redmond at Penguin for flying the American flag; Imogen Fox, Priscilla Kwateng, Stevie Brown, Kelly Bowerbank, Paula Cocozza, Kathy Chan and honorary fashion desk members Ben Clissitt and Simon Chilvers for personal styling and personal therapy. Sophia Neophitou, Antony Miles and Dan May for never telling me to shut up; my family for never doubting the veracity of my opinions in spite of all evidence to the contrary; Carol Miller, Charlie Porter, the Ibizans, Marina Hyde, Simon Woods, Jamie Dornan, Poppy de Villeneuve, Sally Henderson, Catherine Boyd, Myles MacInnes, Conrad Shawcross, Patrick Kennedy, Martin Tisne, Tessa Bilder and Helen Seamons for always ensuring I get home safely at the end of the night.

You're all fabulous. Mwah.